NumPy Beginner's Guide
Second Edition

An action packed guide using real world examples of the
easy to use, high performance, free open source NumPy
mathematical library

Ivan Idris

[PACKT]
PUBLISHING

open source *
community experience distilled

BIRMINGHAM - MUMBAI

Numpy Beginner's Guide
Second Edition

First published: November 2011
Second edition: April 2013

Production Reference: 1170413

Published by Packt Publishing Ltd.
Livery Place
35 Livery Street
Birmingham B3 2PB, UK.

ISBN 978-1-78216-608-5

www.packtpub.com

Cover Image by Suresh Mogre (suresh.mogre.99@gmail.com)

Credits

Author

Ivan Idris

Reviewers

Jaidev Deshpande

Dr. Alexandre Devert

Mark Livingstone

Miklós Prisznyák

Nikolay Karelin

Acquisition Editor

Usha Iyer

Lead Technical Editor

Joel Noronha

Technical Editors

Soumya Kanti

Devdutt Kulkarni

Project Coordinator

Abhishek Kori

Proofreader

Mario Cecere

Indexer

Hemangini Bari

Graphics

Sheetal Aute

Ronak Dhruv

Production Coordinator

Melwyn D'sa

Cover Work

Melwyn D'sa

About the Author

Ivan Idris has an MSc in Experimental Physics. His graduation thesis had a strong emphasis on Applied Computer Science. After graduating, he worked for several companies as a Java Developer, Datawarehouse Developer, and QA Analyst. His main professional interests are Business Intelligence, Big Data, and Cloud Computing. Ivan Idris enjoys writing clean testable code and interesting technical articles. Ivan Idris is the author of NumPy Beginner's Guide & Cookbook. You can find more information and a blog with a few NumPy examples at ivanidris.net.

I would like to take this opportunity to thank the reviewers and the team at Packt Publishing for making this book possible. Also thanks goes to my teachers, professors, and colleagues who taught me about science and programming. Last but not the least, I would like to acknowledge my parents, family, and friends for their support.

About the Reviewers

Jaidev Deshpande is an intern at Enthought, Inc, where he works on software for data analysis and visualization. He is an avid scientific programmer and works on many open source packages in signal processing, data analysis, and machine learning.

Dr. Alexandre Devert is teaching data-mining and software engineering at the University of Science and Technology of China. Alexandre also works as a researcher, both as an academic on optimization problems, and on data-mining problems for a biotechnology startup. In all those contexts, Alexandre very happily uses Python, Numpy, and Scipy.

Mark Livingstone started his career by working for many years for three international computer companies (which no longer exist) in engineering/support/programming/training roles, but got tired of being made redundant. He then graduated from Griffith University on the Gold Coast, Australia, in 2011 with a Bachelor of Information Technology. He is currently in his final semester of his B.InfoTech (Hons) degree researching in the area of Proteomics algorithms with all his research software written in Python on a Mac, and his Supervisor and research group one by one discovering the joys of Python.

Mark enjoys mentoring first year students with special needs, is the Chair of the IEEE Griffith University Gold Coast Student Branch, and volunteers as a Qualified Justice of the Peace at the local District Courthouse, has been a Credit Union Director, and will have completed 100 blood donations by the end of 2013.

In his copious spare time, he co-develops the S2 Salstat Statistics Package available at `http://code.google.com/p/salstat-statistics-package-2/` which is multiplatform and uses wxPython, NumPy, SciPy, Scikit, Matplotlib, and a number of other Python modules.

Miklós Prisznyák is a senior software engineer with a scientific background. He graduated as a physicist from the Eötvös Lóránd University, the largest and oldest university in Hungary. He did his MSc thesis on Monte Carlo simulations of non-Abelian lattice quantum field theories in 1992. Having worked three years in the Central Research Institute for Physics of Hungary, he joined MultiRáció Kft. in Budapest, a company founded by physicists, which specialized in mathematical data analysis and forecasting economic data. His main project was the Small Area Unemployment Statistics System which has been in official use at the Hungarian Public Employment Service since then. He learned about the Python programming language here in 2000. He set up his own consulting company in 2002 and then he worked on various projects for insurance, pharmacy and e-commerce companies, using Python whenever he could. He also worked in a European Union research institute in Italy, testing and enhancing a distributed, Python-based Zope/Plone web application. He moved to Great Britain in 2007 and first he worked at a Scottish start-up, using Twisted Python, then in the aerospace industry in England using, among others, the PyQt windowing toolkit, the Enthought application framework, and the NumPy and SciPy libraries. He returned to Hungary in 2012 and he rejoined MultiRáció where now he is working on a Python extension module to OpenOffice/EuroOffice, using NumPy and SciPy again, which will allow users to solve non-linear and stochastic optimization problems. Miklós likes to travel, read, and he is interested in sciences, linguistics, history, politics, the board game of go, and in quite a few other topics. Besides he always enjoys a good cup of coffee. However, nothing beats spending time with his brilliant 10 year old son Zsombor for him.

Nikolay Karelin holds a PhD degree in optics and used various methods of numerical simulations and analysis for nearly 20 years, first in academia and then in the industry (simulation of fiber optics communication links). After initial learning curve with Python and NumPy, these excellent tools became his main choice for almost all numerical analysis and scripting, since past five years.

> I wish to thank my family for understanding and keeping patience during long evenings when I was working on reviews for the "NumPy Beginner's Guide."

www.PacktPub.com

Support files, eBooks, discount offers and more

You might want to visit www.PacktPub.com for support files and downloads related to your book.

Did you know that Packt offers eBook versions of every book published, with PDF and ePub files available? You can upgrade to the eBook version at www.PacktPub.com and as a print book customer, you are entitled to a discount on the eBook copy. Get in touch with us at service@packtpub.com for more details.

At www.PacktPub.com, you can also read a collection of free technical articles, sign up for a range of free newsletters and receive exclusive discounts and offers on Packt books and eBooks.

http://PacktLib.PacktPub.com

Do you need instant solutions to your IT questions? PacktLib is Packt's online digital book library. Here, you can access, read and search across Packt's entire library of books.

Why Subscribe?

- Fully searchable across every book published by Packt
- Copy and paste, print and bookmark content
- On demand and accessible via web browser

Free Access for Packt account holders

If you have an account with Packt at www.PacktPub.com, you can use this to access PacktLib today and view nine entirely free books. Simply use your login credentials for immediate access.

To my family and friends.

Table of Contents

Preface

Scientists, engineers, and quantitative data analysts face many challenges nowadays. Data scientists want to be able to do numerical analysis of large datasets with minimal programming effort. They want to write readable, efficient, and fast code, which is as close as possible to the mathematical language package they are used to. A number of accepted solutions are available in the scientific computing world.

The C, C++, and Fortran programming languages have their benefits, but they are not interactive and considered too complex by many. The common commercial alternatives are amongst others, Matlab, Maple and Mathematica. These products provide powerful scripting languages, which are still more limited than any general purpose programming language. Other open source tools similar to Matlab exist such as R, GNU Octave, and Scilab. Obviously, they also lack the power of a language such as Python.

Python is a popular general-purpose programming language, widely used in the scientific community. You can access legacy C, Fortran, or R code easily from Python. It is object-oriented and considered more high level than C or Fortran. Python allows you to write readable and clean code with minimal fuss. However, it lacks a Matlab equivalent out of the box. That's where NumPy comes in. This book is about NumPy and related Python libraries such as SciPy and Matplotlib.

What is NumPy?

NumPy (from Numerical Python) is an open-source Python library for scientific computing. NumPy let's you work with arrays and matrices in a natural way. The library contains a long list of useful mathematical functions including some for linear algebra, Fourier transformation, and random number generation routines. LAPACK, a linear algebra library, is used by the NumPy linear algebra module (that is, if you have LAPACK installed on your system), otherwise, NumPy provides its own implementation. LAPACK is a well-known library originally written in Fortran on which Matlab relies as well. In a sense, NumPy replaces some of the functionality of Matlab and Mathematica, allowing rapid interactive prototyping.

We will not be discussing NumPy from a developing contributor perspective, but more from a user's perspective. NumPy is a very active project and has a lot of contributors. Maybe, one day you will be one of them!

History

NumPy is based on its predecessor Numeric. Numeric was first released in 1995 and has a deprecated status now. Neither Numeric nor NumPy made it into the standard Python library for various reasons. However, you can install NumPy separately as will be explained in *Chapter 1, Numpy Quick Start*.

In 2001, a number of people inspired by Numeric created SciPy—an open-source Python scientific computing library, that provides functionality similar to that of Matlab, Maple, and Mathematica. Around this time, people were growing increasingly unhappy with Numeric. Numarray was created as alternative to Numeric. Numarray was better in some areas than Numeric, but worked very differently. For that reason, SciPy kept on depending on the Numeric philosophy and the Numeric array object. As is customary with new "latest and greatest" software, the arrival of Numarray led to the development of an entire ecosystem around it with a range of useful tools.

In 2005, Travis Oliphant, an early contributor to SciPy, decided to do something about this situation. He tried to integrate some of the Numarray features into Numeric. A complete rewrite took place that culminated in the release of NumPy 1.0 in 2006. At this time, NumPy has all of the features of Numeric and Numarray and more. Upgrade tools are available to facilitate the upgrade from Numeric and Numarray. The upgrade is recommended since Numeric and Numarray are not actively supported any more.

Originally, the NumPy code was part of SciPy. It was later separated and is now used by SciPy for array and matrix processing.

Why use NumPy?

NumPy code is much cleaner than "straight" Python code that tries to accomplish the same task. There are less loops required, because operations work directly on arrays and matrices. The many convenience and mathematical functions make life easier as well. The underlying algorithms have stood the test of time and have been designed with high performance in mind.

NumPy's arrays are stored more efficiently than an equivalent data structure in base Python such as list of lists. Array IO is significantly faster too. The performance improvement scales with the number of elements of an array. For large arrays it really pays off to use NumPy. Files as large as several terabytes can be memory-mapped to arrays, leading to optimal reading and writing of data. The drawback of NumPy arrays is that they are more specialized than plain lists. Outside of the context of numerical computations, NumPy arrays are less useful. The technical details of NumPy arrays will be discussed in the later chapters.

Large portions of NumPy are written in C. That makes NumPy faster than pure Python code. A NumPy C API exists as well and it allows further extension of the functionality with the help of the C language of NumPy. The C API falls outside the scope of this book. Finally, since NumPy is open-source, you get all of the related advantages. The price is the lowest possible—free as in "beer". You don't have to worry about licenses every time somebody joins your team or you need an upgrade of the software. The source code is available to everyone. This of course is beneficial to the code quality.

Limitations of NumPy

If you are a Java programmer, you might be interested in Jython, the Java implementation of Python. In that case, I have bad news for you. Unfortunately, Jython runs on the Java Virtual Machine and cannot access NumPy, because NumPy's modules are mostly written in C. You could say that Jython and Python are two totally different worlds, although, they do implement the same specification. There are some workarounds for this that are discussed in *NumPy Cookbook, Ivan Idris, Packt Publishing*.

What this book covers

Chapter 1, NumPy Quick Start will guide you through the steps needed to install NumPy on your system and create a basic NumPy application.

Chapter 2, Beginning with NumPy Fundamentals introduces you to NumPy arrays and fundamentals.

Chapter 3, Get to Terms with Commonly Used Functions will teach you about the most commonly used NumPy functions—the basic mathematical and statistical functions.

Chapter 4, Convenience Functions for Your Convenience will teach you about functions that make working with NumPy easier. This includes functions that select certain parts of your arrays, for instance, based on a Boolean condition. You will also learn about polynomials, and manipulating the shape of NumPy objects.

Chapter 5, Working with Matrices and ufuncs covers matrices and universal functions. Matrices are well known in mathematics and have their representation in NumPy as well. Universal functions (ufuncs) work on arrays element-by-element or on scalars. Ufuncs expect a set of scalars as input and produce a set of scalars as output.

Chapter 6, Move Further with Numpy Modules discusses the number of basic modules of Universal functions. Universal functions can typically be mapped to mathematical counterparts such as add, subtract, divide, and multiply.

Chapter 7, Peeking into Special Routines describes some of the more specialized NumPy functions. As NumPy users, we sometimes find ourselves having special needs. Fortunately, NumPy provides for most of our needs.

In *Chapter 8, Assure Quality with Testing* you will learn how to write NumPy unit tests.

Chapter 9, Plotting with Matplotlib covers in-depth Matplotlib, a very useful Python plotting library. NumPy on its own cannot be used to create graphs and plots. But Matplotlib integrates nicely with NumPy and has plotting capabilities comparable to Matlab.

Chapter 10, When NumPy is Not Enough – SciPy and Beyond goes into more detail about SciPy, we know that SciPy and NumPy are historically related. SciPy, as mentioned in the *History* section, is a high level Python scientific computing framework built on top of NumPy. It can be used in conjunction with NumPy.

Chapter 11, Playing with Pygame is the dessert of this book. We will learn how to create fun games with NumPy and Pygame. We also get a taste of artificial intelligence.

What you need for this book

To try out the code samples in this book you will need a recent build of NumPy. This means that you will need to have one of the Python versions supported by NumPy as well. Some code samples make use of the Matplotlib for illustration purposes. Matplotlib is not strictly required to follow the examples, but it is recommended that you install it too. The last chapter is about SciPy and has one example involving Scikits.

Here is a list of software used to develop and test the code examples:

- Python 2.7
- NumPy 2.0.0.dev20100915
- SciPy 0.9.0.dev20100915
- Matplotlib 1.1.1
- Pygame 1.9.1
- IPython 0.14.dev

Needless to say, you don't need to have exactly this software and these versions on your computer. Python and NumPy is the absolute minimum you will need.

Who this book is for

This book is for you the scientist, engineer, programmer, or analyst, looking for a high quality open source mathematical library. Knowledge of Python is assumed. Also, some affinity or at least interest in mathematics and statistics is required.

Conventions

In this book, you will find a number of styles of text that distinguish between different kinds of information. Here are some examples of these styles, and an explanation of their meaning.

Code words in text are shown as follows: "Notice that `numpysum()` does not need a `for` loop."

A block of code is set as follows:

```
def numpysum(n):
    a = numpy.arange(n) ** 2
    b = numpy.arange(n) ** 3
    c = a + b
    return c
```

When we wish to draw your attention to a particular part of a code block, the relevant lines or items are set in bold:

```
reals = np.isreal(xpoints)
print "Real number?", reals
Real number? [ True   True   True   True False False False False]
```

Any command-line input or output is written as follows:

```
>>>fromnumpy.testing import rundocs
>>>rundocs('docstringtest.py')
```

New terms and **important words** are shown in bold. Words that you see on the screen, in menus or dialog boxes for example, appear in the text like this: "clicking the **Next** button moves you to the next screen".

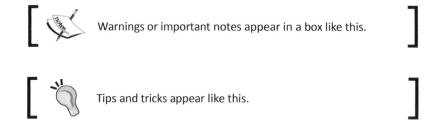

[Warnings or important notes appear in a box like this.]

[Tips and tricks appear like this.]

Reader feedback

Feedback from our readers is always welcome. Let us know what you think about this book—what you liked or may have disliked. Reader feedback is important for us to develop titles that you really get the most out of.

To send us general feedback, simply send an e-mail to feedback@packtpub.com, and mention the book title via the subject of your message.

If there is a book that you need and would like to see us publish, please send us a note in the **SUGGEST A TITLE** form on www.packtpub.com or e-mail suggest@packtpub.com.

If there is a topic that you have expertise in and you are interested in either writing or contributing to a book, see our author guide on www.packtpub.com/authors.

Customer support

Now that you are the proud owner of a Packt book, we have a number of things to help you to get the most from your purchase.

Downloading the example code

You can download the example code files for all Packt books you have purchased from your account at http://www.PacktPub.com. If you purchased this book elsewhere, you can visit http://www.PacktPub.com/support and register to have the files e-mailed directly to you.

Errata

Although we have taken every care to ensure the accuracy of our content, mistakes do happen. If you find a mistake in one of our books—maybe a mistake in the text or the code—we would be grateful if you would report this to us. By doing so, you can save other readers from frustration and help us improve subsequent versions of this book. If you find any errata, please report them by visiting `http://www.packtpub.com/support`, selecting your book, clicking on the **errata submission form** link, and entering the details of your errata. Once your errata are verified, your submission will be accepted and the errata will be uploaded on our website, or added to any list of existing errata, under the Errata section of that title. Any existing errata can be viewed by selecting your title from `http://www.packtpub.com/support`.

Piracy

Piracy of copyright material on the Internet is an ongoing problem across all media. At Packt, we take the protection of our copyright and licenses very seriously. If you come across any illegal copies of our works, in any form, on the Internet, please provide us with the location address or website name immediately so that we can pursue a remedy.

Please contact us at `copyright@packtpub.com` with a link to the suspected pirated material.

We appreciate your help in protecting our authors, and our ability to bring you valuable content.

Questions

You can contact us at `questions@packtpub.com` if you are having a problem with any aspect of the book, and we will do our best to address it.

1

NumPy Quick Start

Let's get started. We will install NumPy and related software on different operating systems and have a look at some simple code that uses NumPy. The IPython interactive shell is introduced briefly. As mentioned in the Preface, SciPy is closely related to NumPy, so you will see the SciPy name appearing here and there. At the end of this chapter, you will find pointers on how to find additional information online if you get stuck or are uncertain about the best way to solve problems.

In this chapter, we shall:

◆   Install Python, SciPy, Matplotlib, IPython, and NumPy on Windows, Linux, and Macintosh

◆   Write simple NumPy code

◆   Get to know IPython

◆   Browse online documentation and resources

Python

NumPy is based on Python, so it is required to have Python installed. On some operating systems, Python is already installed. However, you need to check whether the Python version corresponds with the NumPy version you want to install. There are many implementations of Python, including commercial implementations and distribution. In this book we will focus on the standard CPython implementation, which is guaranteed to be compatible with NumPy.

Time for action – installing Python on different operating systems

NumPy has binary installers for Windows, various Linux distributions, and Mac OS X. There is also a source distribution, if you prefer that. You need to have Python 2.4.x or above installed on your system. We will go through the various steps required to install Python on the following operating systems:

1. **Debian and Ubuntu**: Python might already be installed on Debian and Ubuntu but the development headers are usually not. On Debian and Ubuntu install python and python-dev with the following commands:

   ```
   sudo apt-get install python
   sudo apt-get install python-dev
   ```

2. **Windows**: The Windows Python installer can be found at `www.python.org/download`. On this website, we can also find installers for Mac OS X and source tarballs for Linux, Unix, and Mac OS X.

3. **Mac**: Python comes pre-installed on Mac OS X. We can also get Python through MacPorts, Fink, or similar projects. We can install, for instance, the Python 2.7 port by running the following command:

   ```
   sudo port install python27
   ```

   `LAPACK` does not need to be present but, if it is, NumPy will detect it and use it during the installation phase. It is recommended to install `LAPACK` for serious numerical analysis as it has useful numerical linear algebra functionality.

What just happened?

We installed Python on Debian, Ubuntu, Windows, and the Mac.

Windows

Installing NumPy on Windows is straightforward. You only need to download an installer, and a wizard will guide you through the installation steps.

Time for action – installing NumPy, Matplotlib, SciPy, and IPython on Windows

Installing NumPy on Windows is necessary but, fortunately, a straightforward task that we will cover in detail. It is recommended to install Matplotlib, SciPy, and IPython. However, this is not required to enjoy this book. The actions we will take are as follows:

1. Download a NumPy installer for Windows from the SourceForge website `http://sourceforge.net/projects/numpy/files/`.

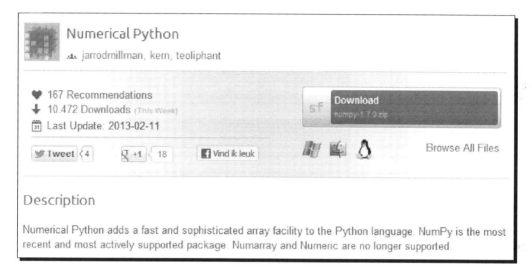

Choose the appropriate version. In this example, we chose `numpy-1.7.0-win32-superpack-python2.7.exe`.

2. Open the EXE installer by double clicking on it.

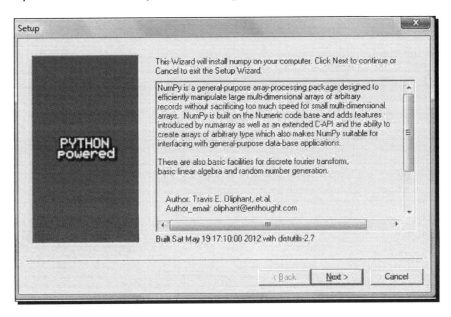

3. Now, we can see a description of NumPy and its features as shown in the previous screenshot. Click on the **Next** button.

4. If you have Python installed, it should automatically be detected. If it is not detected, maybe your path settings are wrong. At the end of this chapter, resources are listed in case you have problems installing NumPy.

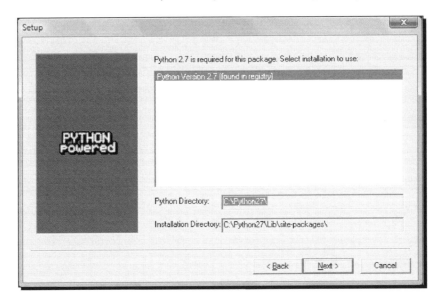

5. In this example, Python 2.7 was found. Click on the **Next** button if Python is found; otherwise, click on the **Cancel** button and install Python (NumPy cannot be installed without Python). Click on the **Next** button. This is the point of no return. Well, kind of, but it is best to make sure that you are installing to the proper directory and so on and so forth. Now the real installation starts. This may take a while.

6. Install SciPy and Matplotlib with the Enthought distribution `http://www.enthought.com/products/epd.php`. It might be necessary to put the `msvcp71.dll` file in your `C:\Windows\system32` directory. You can get it from `http://www.dll-files.com/dllindex/dll-files.shtml?msvcp71`. A Windows IPython installer is available on the IPython website (see `http://ipython.scipy.org/Wiki/IpythonOnWindows`).

What just happened?

We installed NumPy, SciPy, Matplotlib, and IPython on Windows.

Linux

Installing NumPy and related recommended software on Linux depends on the distribution you have. We will discuss how you would install NumPy from the command line, although, you could probably use graphical installers; it depends on your distribution (distro). The commands to install Matplotlib, SciPy, and IPython are the same – only the package names are different. Installing Matplotlib, SciPy, and IPython is recommended, but optional.

Time for action – installing NumPy, Matplotlib, SciPy, and IPython on Linux

Most Linux distributions have NumPy packages. We will go through the necessary steps for some of the popular Linux distros:

1. Run the following instructions from the command line for installing NumPy and Red Hat:

   ```
   yum install python-numpy
   ```

2. To install NumPy on Mandriva, run the following command-line instruction:

   ```
   urpmi python-numpy
   ```

3. To install NumPy on Gentoo run the following command-line instruction:

   ```
   sudo emerge numpy
   ```

4. To install NumPy on Debian or Ubuntu, we need to type the following :

```
sudo apt-get install python-numpy
```

The following table gives an overview of the Linux distributions and corresponding package names for NumPy, SciPy, Matplotlib, and IPython.

Linux distribution	NumPy	SciPy	Matplotlib	IPython
Arch Linux	python-numpy	python-scipy	python-matplotlib	ipython
Debian	python-numpy	python-scipy	python-matplotlib	ipython
Fedora	numpy	python-scipy	python-matplotlib	ipython
Gentoo	dev-python/numpy	scipy	matplotlib	ipython
OpenSUSE	python-numpy, python-numpy-devel	python-scipy	python-matplotlib	ipython
Slackware	numpy	scipy	matplotlib	ipython

What just happened?

We installed NumPy, SciPy, Matplotlib, and IPython on various Linux distributions.

Mac OS X

You can install NumPy, Matplotlib, and SciPy on the Mac with a graphical installer or from the command line with a port manager such as MacPorts or Fink, depending on your preference.

Time for action – installing NumPy, Matplotlib, and SciPy on Mac OS X

We will install NumPy with a GUI installer using the following steps:

1. We can get a NumPy installer from the SourceForge website `http://sourceforge.net/projects/numpy/files/`. Similar files exist for Matplotlib and SciPy. Just change `numpy` in the previous URL to `scipy` or `matplotlib`. IPython didn't have a GUI installer at the time of writing. Download the appropriate DMG file as shown in the following screenshot, usually the latest one is the best:

Looking for the latest version? **Download numpy-1.7.0.zip (3.1 MB)**				
Home				f
Name ◆	**Modified** ◆	**Size** ◆	**Downloads** ◆	
o **NumPy**	2013-02-10			◣
o **Old Numarray**	2006-08-24			☐
o **Old Numeric**	2005-11-13			☐
Totals: 3 Items				

2. Open the DMG file as shown in the following screenshot (in this example, `numpy-1.7.0-py2.7-python.org-macosx10.6.dmg`):

□ Double-click on the icon of the opened box, the one having a subscript that ends with **.mpkg**. We will be presented with the welcome screen of the installer.

❏ Click on the **Continue** button to go to the **Read Me** screen, where we will be presented with a short description of NumPy as shown in the following screenshot:

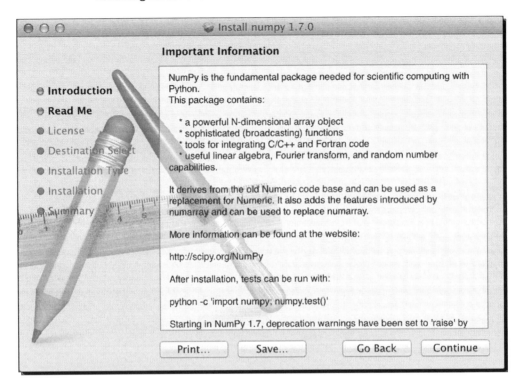

❏ Click on the **Continue** button to the License the screen.

3. Read the license, click on the **Continue** button and then on the **Accept** button, when prompted to accept the license. Continue through the next screens and click on the **Finish** button at the end.

What just happened?

We installed NumPy on Mac OS X with a GUI installer. The steps to install SciPy and Matplotlib are similar and can be performed using the URLs mentioned in the first step.

Time for action – installing NumPy, SciPy, Matplotlib, and IPython with MacPorts or Fink

Alternatively, we can install NumPy, SciPy, Matplotlib, and IPython through the MacPorts route or with Fink. The following installation steps shown install all these packages. We only need NumPy for all the tutorials in this book, so please omit the packages you are not interested in.

1. For installing with MacPorts, type the following command:

   ```
   sudo port install py-numpy py-scipy py-matplotlib py-ipython
   ```

2. Fink also has packages for NumPy: scipy-core-py24, scipy-core-py25, and scipy-core-py26. The SciPy packages are: scipy-py24, scipy-py25, and scipy-py26. We can install NumPy and the other recommended packages we will be using in this book for Python 2.6 with the following command:

   ```
   fink install scipy-core-py26 scipy-py26 matplotlib-py26
   ```

What just happened?

We installed NumPy and other recommended software on Mac OS X with MacPorts and Fink.

Building from source

We can retrieve the source code for NumPy with git as follows:

```
git clone git://github.com/numpy/numpy.git numpy
```

Install /usr/local with the following command:

```
python setup.py build
sudo python setup.py install --prefix=/usr/local
```

To build, we need a C compiler such as GCC and the Python header files in the python-dev or python-devel package.

Arrays

After going through the installation of NumPy, it's time to have a look at NumPy arrays. NumPy arrays are more efficient than Python lists, when it comes to numerical operations. NumPy code requires less explicit loops than equivalent Python code.

Time for action – adding vectors

Imagine that we want to add two vectors called a and b. Vector is used here in the mathematical sense meaning a one-dimensional array. We will learn in *Chapter 5, Working with Matrices and ufuncs*, about specialized NumPy arrays which represent matrices. The vector a holds the squares of integers 0 to *n*, for instance, if n is equal to 3, then a is equal to 0, 1, or 4. The vector b holds the cubes of integers 0 to *n*, so if n is equal to 3, then the vector b is equal to 0, 1, or 8. How would you do that using plain Python? After we come up with a solution, we will compare it with the NumPy equivalent.

1. The following function solves the vector addition problem using pure Python without NumPy:

```
def pythonsum(n):
    a = range(n)
    b = range(n)
    c = []

    for i in range(len(a)):
        a[i] = i ** 2
        b[i] = i ** 3
        c.append(a[i] + b[i])

    return c
```

2. The following is a function that achieves the same with NumPy:

```
def numpysum(n):
    a = numpy.arange(n) ** 2
    b = numpy.arange(n) ** 3
    c = a + b
    return c
```

Notice that numpysum() does not need a for loop. Also, we used the arange function from NumPy that creates a NumPy array for us with integers 0 to *n*. The arange function was imported; that is why it is prefixed with numpy.

Now comes the fun part. Remember that it is mentioned in the *Preface* that NumPy is faster when it comes to array operations. How much faster is Numpy, though? The following program will show us by measuring the elapsed time in microseconds, for the numpysum and pythonsum functions. It also prints the last two elements of the vector sum. Let's check that we get the same answers by using Python and NumPy:

```
#!/usr/bin/env/python

import sys
```

```
from datetime import datetime
import numpy as np

"""
 Chapter 1 of NumPy Beginners Guide.
 This program demonstrates vector addition the Python way.
 Run from the command line as follows

  python vectorsum.py n

 where n is an integer that specifies the size of the vectors.

 The first vector to be added contains the squares of 0 up to n.
 The second vector contains the cubes of 0 up to n.
 The program prints the last 2 elements of the sum and the elapsed
time.
"""

def numpysum(n):
    a = np.arange(n) ** 2
    b = np.arange(n) ** 3
    c = a + b

    return c

def pythonsum(n):
    a = range(n)
    b = range(n)
    c = []

    for i in range(len(a)):
        a[i] = i ** 2
        b[i] = i ** 3
        c.append(a[i] + b[i])

    return c

size = int(sys.argv[1])

start = datetime.now()
c = pythonsum(size)
delta = datetime.now() - start
print "The last 2 elements of the sum", c[-2:]
print "PythonSum elapsed time in microseconds", delta.microseconds
```

```
start = datetime.now()
c = numpysum(size)
delta = datetime.now() - start
print "The last 2 elements of the sum", c[-2:]
print "NumPySum elapsed time in microseconds", delta.microseconds
```

The output of the program for 1000, 2000, and 3000 vector elements is as follows:

```
$ python vectorsum.py 1000
The last 2 elements of the sum [995007996, 998001000]
PythonSum elapsed time in microseconds 707
The last 2 elements of the sum [995007996 998001000]
NumPySum elapsed time in microseconds 171

$ python vectorsum.py 2000
The last 2 elements of the sum [7980015996, 7992002000]
PythonSum elapsed time in microseconds 1420
The last 2 elements of the sum [7980015996 7992002000]
NumPySum elapsed time in microseconds 168

$ python vectorsum.py 4000
The last 2 elements of the sum [63920031996, 63968004000]
PythonSum elapsed time in microseconds 2829
The last 2 elements of the sum [63920031996 63968004000]
NumPySum elapsed time in microseconds 274
```

 You can download the example code files for all Packt books you have purchased from your account at http://www.PacktPub.com. If you purchased this book elsewhere, you can visit http://www.PacktPub.com/support and register to have the files e-mailed directly to you.

What just happened?

Clearly, NumPy is much faster than the equivalent normal Python code. One thing is certain; we get the same results whether we are using NumPy or not. However, the result that is printed differs in representation. Notice that the result from the numpysum function does not have any commas. How come? Obviously we are not dealing with a Python list but with a NumPy array. It was mentioned in the *Preface* that NumPy arrays are specialized data structures for numerical data. We will learn more about NumPy arrays in the next chapter.

Pop quiz Functioning of the arange function

Q1. What does `arange(5)` do?

1. Creates a Python list of 5 elements with values 1 to 5.

2. Creates a Python list of 5 elements with values 0 to 4.

3. Creates a NumPy array with values 1 to 5.

4. Creates a NumPy array with values 0 to 4.

5. None of the above.

Have a go hero – continue the analysis

The program we used here to compare the speed of NumPy and regular Python is not very scientific. We should at least repeat each measurement a couple of times. It would be nice to be able to calculate some statistics such as average times, and so on. Also, you might want to show plots of the measurements to friends and colleagues.

Hints to help can be found in the online documentation and resources listed at the end of this chapter. NumPy has, by the way, statistical functions that can calculate averages for you. I recommend using Matplotlib to produce plots. *Chapter 9, Plotting with Matplotlib*, gives a quick overview of Matplotlib.

IPython—an interactive shell

Scientists and engineers are used to experimenting. IPython was created by scientists with experimentation in mind. The interactive environment that IPython provides is viewed by many as a direct answer to Matlab, Mathematica, and Maple. You can find more information, including installation instructions, at: `http://ipython.org/`.

IPython is free, open source, and available for Linux, Unix, Mac OS X, and Windows. The IPython authors only request that you cite IPython in scientific work where IPython was used. Here is the list of basic IPython features:

◆ Tab completion

◆ History mechanism

◆ Inline editing

◆ Ability to call external Python scripts with `%run`

- ◆ Access to system commands
- ◆ Pylab switch
- ◆ Access to Python debugger and profiler

The Pylab switch imports all the `Scipy`, `NumPy`, and `Matplotlib` packages. Without this switch, we would have to import every package we need, ourselves.

All we need to do is enter the following instruction on the command line:

```
$ ipython --pylab
Python 2.7.2 (default, Jun 20 2012, 16:23:33)
Type "copyright", "credits" or "license" for more information.


IPython 0.14.dev -- An enhanced Interactive Python.
?           -> Introduction and overview of IPython's features.
%quickref -> Quick reference.
help        -> Python's own help system.
object?    -> Details about 'object', use 'object??' for extra details.


Welcome to pylab, a matplotlib-based Python environment [backend:
MacOSX].
For more information, type 'help(pylab)'.
In [1]: quit()
```

The `quit()` function or *Ctrl + D* quits the IPython shell. We might want to be able to go back to our experiments. In IPython, it is easy to save a session for later:

```
In [1]: %logstart
Activating auto-logging. Current session state plus future input saved.
Filename        : ipython_log.py
Mode            : rotate
Output logging : False
Raw input log  : False
Timestamping   : False
State           : active
```

Let's say we have the vector addition program that we made in the current directory. We can run the script as follows:

```
In [1]: ls
README          vectorsum.py
```

```
In [2]: %run -i vectorsum.py 1000
```

As you probably remember, `1000` specifies the number of elements in a vector. The `-d` switch of `%run` starts an `ipdb` debugger and on typing `c`, the script is started. *n* steps through the code. Typing `quit` at the `ipdb` prompt exits the debugger.

```
In [2]: %run -d vectorsum.py 1000
*** Blank or comment
*** Blank or comment
Breakpoint 1 at: /Users/.../vectorsum.py:3
```

Type c at the `ipdb>` prompt to start your script.

```
><string>(1)<module>()
ipdb> c
> /Users/.../vectorsum.py(3)<module>()
      2
1---> 3 import sys
      4 from datetime import datetime
ipdb> n
>
/Users/.../vectorsum.py(4)<module>()
1      3 import sys
----> 4 from datetime import datetime
      5 import numpy
ipdb> n
> /Users/.../vectorsum.py(5)<module>()
      4 from datetime import datetime
----> 5 import numpy
      6
ipdb> quit
```

We can also profile our script by passing the `-p` option to `%run`.

```
In [4]: %run -p vectorsum.py 1000
        1058 function calls (1054 primitive calls) in 0.002 CPU seconds
   Ordered by: internal time
ncallstottimepercallcumtimepercallfilename:lineno(function)
1 0.001     0.001     0.001      0.001 vectorsum.py:28(pythonsum)
1 0.001     0.001     0.002      0.002 {execfile}
```

```
1000 0.000    0.0000.0000.000 {method 'append' of 'list' objects}
1 0.000     0.000    0.002    0.002 vectorsum.py:3(<module>)
1 0.000     0.0000.0000.000 vectorsum.py:21(numpysum)
3    0.000    0.0000.0000.000 {range}
1    0.000    0.0000.0000.000 arrayprint.py:175(_array2string)
3/1    0.000    0.0000.0000.000 arrayprint.py:246(array2string)
2    0.000    0.0000.0000.000 {method 'reduce' of 'numpy.ufunc' objects}
4    0.000    0.0000.0000.000 {built-in method now}
2    0.000    0.0000.0000.000 arrayprint.py:486(_formatInteger)
2    0.000    0.0000.0000.000 {numpy.core.multiarray.arange}
1    0.000    0.0000.0000.000 arrayprint.py:320(_formatArray)
3/1    0.000    0.0000.0000.000 numeric.py:1390(array_str)
1    0.000    0.0000.0000.000 numeric.py:216(asarray)
2    0.000    0.0000.0000.000 arrayprint.py:312(_extendLine)
1    0.000    0.0000.0000.000 fromnumeric.py:1043(ravel)
2    0.000    0.0000.0000.000 arrayprint.py:208(<lambda>)
1    0.000    0.000    0.002    0.002<string>:1(<module>)
11    0.000    0.0000.0000.000 {len}
2    0.000    0.0000.0000.000 {isinstance}
1    0.000    0.0000.0000.000 {reduce}
1    0.000    0.0000.0000.000 {method 'ravel' of 'numpy.ndarray' objects}
4    0.000    0.0000.0000.000 {method 'rstrip' of 'str' objects}
3    0.000    0.0000.0000.000 {issubclass}
2    0.000    0.0000.0000.000 {method 'item' of 'numpy.ndarray' objects}
1    0.000    0.0000.0000.000 {max}
1    0.000    0.0000.0000.000 {method 'disable' of '_lsprof.Profiler'
objects}
```

This gives us a bit more insight into the workings of our program. In addition, we can now identify performance bottlenecks. The `%hist` command shows the commands history.

```
In [2]: a=2+2
In [3]: a
Out[3]: 4
In [4]: %hist
1: _ip.magic("hist ")
2: a=2+2
3: a
```

I hope you agree that IPython is a really useful tool!

Online resources and help

When we are in IPython's pylab mode, we can open manual pages for `NumPy` functions with the `help` command. It is not necessary to know the name of a function. We can type a few characters and then let tab completion do its work. Let's, for instance, browse the available information for the `arange` function.

```
In [2]: help ar<Tab>
```

arange	arctan	argsort	array_equal	arrow
arccos	arctan2	argwhere	array_equiv	
arccosh	arctanh	around	array_repr	
arcsin	argmax	array	array_split	
arcsinh	argmin	array2string	array_str	

```
In [2]: help arange
```

Another option is to put a question mark behind the function name:

```
In [3]: arange?
```

The main documentation website for NumPy and SciPy is at `http://docs.scipy.org/doc/`. Through this webpage, we can browse the NumPy reference at `http://docs.scipy.org/doc/numpy/reference/` and the user guide as well as several tutorials.

NumPy has a wiki with lots of documentation at `http://docs.scipy.org/numpy/Front%20Page/`.

The NumPy and SciPy forum can be found at `http://ask.scipy.org/en`.

The popular Stack Overflow software development forum has hundreds of questions tagged `numpy`. To view them, go to `http://stackoverflow.com/questions/tagged/numpy`.

If you are really stuck with a problem or you want to be kept informed of NumPy development, you can subscribe to the NumPy discussion mailing list. The e-mail address is `numpy-discussion@scipy.org`. The number of e-mails per day is not too high and there is almost no spam to speak of. Most importantly, developers actively involved with NumPy also answer questions asked on the discussion group. The complete list can be found at `http://www.scipy.org/Mailing_Lists`.

For IRC users, there is an IRC channel on `irc.freenode.net`. The channel is called `#scipy`, but you can also ask NumPy questions since SciPy users also have knowledge of NumPy, as SciPy is based on NumPy. There are at least 50 members on the SciPy channel at all times.

Summary

In this chapter, we installed NumPy and other recommended software that we will be using in some tutorials. We got a vector addition program working and convinced ourselves that NumPy has superior performance. We were introduced to the IPython interactive shell. In addition, we explored the available NumPy documentation and online resources.

In the next chapter, we will take a look under the hood and explore some fundamental concepts including arrays and data types.

2

Beginning with NumPy Fundamentals

After installing NumPy and getting some code to work, it's time to cover NumPy basics.

The topics we shall cover in this chapter are:

- ◆ Data types
- ◆ Array types
- ◆ Type conversions
- ◆ Array creation
- ◆ Indexing
- ◆ Slicing
- ◆ Shape manipulation

Before we start, let me make a few remarks about the code examples in this chapter. The code snippets in this chapter show input and output from several IPython sessions. Recall that IPython was introduced in *Chapter 1*, *NumPy Quick Start*, as the interactive Python shell of choice for scientific computing. The advantages of IPython are the PyLab switch that imports many scientific computing Python packages, including NumPy, and the fact that it is not necessary to explicitly call the `print` function to display variable values. However, the source code delivered alongside the book is regular Python code that uses `imports` and `print` statements.

NumPy array object

NumPy has a multi-dimensional array object called `ndarray`. It consists of two parts:

- The actual data
- Some metadata describing the data

The majority of array operations leave the raw data untouched. The only aspect that changes is the metadata.

We have already learned, in the previous chapter, how to create an array using the `arange` function. Actually, we created a one-dimensional array that contained a set of numbers. `ndarray` can have more than one dimension.

The NumPy array is in general homogeneous (there is a special array type that is heterogeneous)—the items in the array have to be of the same type. The advantage is that, if we know that the items in the array are of the same type, it is easy to determine the storage size required for the array.

NumPy arrays are indexed just like in Python, starting from 0. Data types are represented by special objects. These objects will be discussed comprehensively in this chapter.

We will create an array with the `arange` function again. Here's how to get the data type of an array:

```
In: a = arange(5)
In: a.dtype
Out: dtype('int64')
```

The data type of array `a` is `int64` (at least on my machine), but you may get `int32` as output if you are using 32-bit Python. In both cases, we are dealing with integers (64-bit or 32-bit). Besides the data type of an array, it is important to know its shape.

The example in *Chapter 1, NumPy Quick Start*, demonstrated how to create a vector (actually, a one-dimensional NumPy array). A vector is commonly used in mathematics but, most of the time, we need higher-dimensional objects. Let's determine the shape of the vector we created a few minutes ago:

```
In [4]: a
Out[4]: array([0, 1, 2, 3, 4])
In: a.shape
Out: (5,)
```

As you can see, the vector has five elements with values ranging from 0 to 4. The shape attribute of the array is a tuple, in this case a tuple of 1 element, which contains the length in each dimension.

Time for action – creating a multidimensional array

Now that we know how to create a vector, we are ready to create a multidimensional NumPy array. After we create the matrix, we would again want to display its shape.

1. Create a multidimensional array.

2. Show the array shape:

```
In: m = array([arange(2), arange(2)])
In: m
Out:
array([[0, 1],
       [0, 1]])
In: m.shape
Out: (2, 2)
```

What just happened?

We created a two-by-two array with the `arange` function we have come to trust and love. Without any warning, the `array` function appeared on the stage.

The `array` function creates an array from an object that you give to it. The object needs to be array-like, for instance, a Python list. In the preceding example, we passed in a list of arrays. The object is the only required argument of the `array` function. NumPy functions tend to have a lot of optional arguments with predefined defaults.

Pop quiz – the shape of ndarray

Q1. How is the shape of an `ndarray` stored?

1. It is stored in a comma-separated string.

2. It is stored in a list.

3. It is stored in a tuple.

Have a go hero – create a three-by-three matrix

It shouldn't be too hard now to create a three-by-three matrix. Give it a go and check whether the array shape is as expected.

Selecting elements

From time to time, we will want to select a particular element of an array. We will take a look at how to do this, but first, let's create a two-by-two matrix again:

```
In: a = array([[1,2],[3,4]])
In: a
Out:
array([[1, 2],
       [3, 4]])
```

The matrix was created this time by passing the `array` function a list of lists. We will now select each item of the matrix one-by-one. Remember, the indices are numbered starting from 0.

```
In: a[0,0]
Out: 1
In: a[0,1]
Out: 2
In: a[1,0]
Out: 3
In: a[1,1]
Out: 4
```

As you can see, selecting elements of the array is pretty simple. For the array `a`, we just use the notation `a[m,n]`, where `m` and `n` are the indices of the item in the array as shown in the following diagram:

NumPy numerical types

Python has an integer type, a float type, and a complex type, however, this is not enough for scientific computing and, for this reason, NumPy has a lot more data types. In practice, we need even more types with varying precision and, therefore, different memory size of the type. The majority of the NumPy numerical types end with a number. This number indicates the number of bits associated with the type. The following table (adapted from the NumPy user guide) gives an overview of NumPy numerical types:

Type	Description
bool	Boolean (True or False) stored as a bit
inti	Platform integer (normally either int32 or int64)
int8	Byte (-128 to 127)
int16	Integer (-32768 to 32767)
int32	Integer (-2 ** 31 to 2 ** 31 -1)
int64	Integer (-2 ** 63 to 2 ** 63 -1)
uint8	Unsigned integer (0 to 255)
uint16	Unsigned integer (0 to 65535)
uint32	Unsigned integer (0 to 2 ** 32 - 1)
uint64	Unsigned integer (0 to 2 ** 64 - 1)
float16	Half precision float: sign bit, 5 bits exponent, 10 bits mantissa
float32	Single precision float: sign bit, 8 bits exponent, 23 bits mantissa
float64 or float	Double precision float: sign bit, 11 bits exponent, 52 bits mantissa
complex64	Complex number, represented by two 32-bit floats (real and imaginary components)
complex128 or complex	Complex number, represented by two 64-bit floats (real and imaginary components)

For each data type, there exists a corresponding conversion function:

```
In: float64(42)
Out: 42.0
In: int8(42.0)
Out: 42
In: bool(42)
Out: True
In: bool(0)
Out: False
In: bool(42.0)
Out: True
In: float(True)
Out: 1.0
In: float(False)
Out: 0.0
```

Many functions have a data type argument, which is often optional:

```
In: arange(7, dtype=uint16)
Out: array([0, 1, 2, 3, 4, 5, 6], dtype=uint16)
```

It is important to know that you are not allowed to convert a complex number into an integer. Trying to do that triggers a **TypeError**:

```
In [1] : int(42.0+1.j)
-----------------------------------------------
TypeError
<ipython-input-1-5e824780381a> in <modu
-------> 1 int(42.0.+1.j)
TypeError: can't convert complex to int
```

The same goes for conversion of a complex number into a float. By the way, the j part is the imaginary coefficient of the complex number. However, you can convert a float to a complex number, for instance complex(1.0).

Data type objects

Data type objects are instances of the numpy.dtype class. Once again, arrays have a data type. To be precise, every element in a NumPy array has the same data type. The data type object can tell you the size of the data in bytes. The size in bytes is given by the itemsize attribute of the dtype class:

```
In: a.dtype.itemsize
Out: 8
```

Character codes

Character codes are included for backward compatibility with Numeric. Numeric is the predecessor of NumPy. Their use is not recommended, but the codes are provided here because they pop up in several places. You should instead use dtype objects.

Type	Character code
integer	i
Unsigned integer	u
Single precision float	f
Double precision float	d
bool	b
complex	D
string	S

Type	Character code
unicode	U
Void	V

Look at the following code to create an array of single precision floats:

```
In: arange(7, dtype='f')
Out: array([ 0.,  1.,  2.,  3.,  4.,  5.,  6.], dtype=float32)
Likewise this creates an array of complex numbers
In: arange(7, dtype='D')
Out: array([ 0.+0.j,  1.+0.j,  2.+0.j,  3.+0.j,  4.+0.j,  5.+0.j,
6.+0.j])
```

dtype constructors

We have a variety of ways to create data types. Take the case of floating point data:

◆ We can use the general Python float:

```
In: dtype(float)
Out: dtype('float64')
```

◆ We can specify a single precision float with a character code:

```
In: dtype('f')
Out: dtype('float32')
```

◆ We can use a double precision float character code:

```
In: dtype('d')
Out: dtype('float64')
```

◆ We can give the data type constructor a two-character code. The first character signifies the type; the second character is a number specifying the number of bytes in the type (the numbers 2, 4 and 8 correspond to 16, 32 and 64 bit floats):

```
In: dtype('f8')
Out: dtype('float64')
```

A listing of all full data type names can be found in `sctypeDict.keys()`:

```
In: sctypeDict.keys()
Out: [0, …
 'i2',
 'int0']
```

dtype attributes

The `dtype` class has a number of useful attributes. For example, we can get information about the character code of a data type through the attributes of `dtype`:

```
In: t = dtype('Float64')
In: t.char
Out: 'd'
```

The type attribute corresponds to the type of object of the array elements:

```
In: t.type
Out: <type 'numpy.float64'>
```

The `str` attribute of `dtype` gives a string representation of the data type. It starts with a character representing endianness, if appropriate, then a character code, followed by a number corresponding to the number of bytes that each array item requires. Endianness, here, means the way bytes are ordered within a 32 or 64-bit word. In big-endian order, the most significant byte is stored first; indicated by >. In little-endian order, the least significant byte is stored first; indicated by <:

```
In: t.str
Out: '<f8'
```

Time for action – creating a record data type

The record data type is a heterogeneous data type—think of it as representing a row in a spreadsheet or a database. To give an example of a record data type, we will create a record for a shop inventory. The record contains the name of the item, a 40-character string, the number of items in the store represented by a 32-bit integer and, finally, a price represented by a 32-bit float. The following steps show how to create a record data type:

1. **Create the record:**

    ```
    In: t = dtype([('name', str_, 40), ('numitems', int32), ('price',
    float32)])
    In: t
    Out: dtype([('name', '|S40'), ('numitems', '<i4'), ('price',
    '<f4')])
    ```

2. View the type (we can view the type of a field as well):

    ```
    In: t['name']
    Out: dtype('|S40')
    ```

If you don't give the `array` function a data type, it will assume that it is dealing with floating point numbers. To create the array now, we really have to specify the data type; otherwise, we will get a `TypeError`:

```
In: itemz = array([('Meaning of life DVD', 42, 3.14), ('Butter', 13, 2.72)], dtype=t)
In: itemz[1]
Out: ('Butter', 13, 2.7200000286102295)
```

What just happened?

We created a record data type, which is a heterogeneous data type. The record contained a name as a character string, a number as an integer and a price represented by a float.

One-dimensional slicing and indexing

Slicing of one-dimensional NumPy arrays works just like slicing of Python lists. We can select a piece of an array from index 3 to 7 that extracts the elements 3 through 6:

```
In: a = arange(9)
In: a[3:7]
Out: array([3, 4, 5, 6])
```

We can select elements from index 0 to 7 with a step of 2:

```
In: a[:7:2]
Out: array([0, 2, 4, 6])
```

Similarly as in Python, we can use negative indices and reverse the array:

```
In: a[::-1]
Out: array([8, 7, 6, 5, 4, 3, 2, 1, 0])
```

Time for action – slicing and indexing multidimensional arrays

A `ndarray` supports slicing over multiple dimensions. For convenience, we refer to many dimensions at once, with an ellipsis.

1. To illustrate, we will create an array with the `arange` function and reshape it:

```
In: b = arange(24).reshape(2,3,4)
In: b.shape
Out: (2, 3, 4)
In: b
Out:
array([[[ 0,  1,  2,  3],
```

```
       [ 4,   5,   6,   7],
       [ 8,   9,  10,  11]],

      [[12,  13,  14,  15],
       [16,  17,  18,  19],
       [20,  21,  22,  23]]])
```

The array b has 24 elements with values 0 to 23 and we reshaped it to be a two-by-three-by-four, three-dimensional array. We can visualize this as a two-story building with 12 rooms on each floor, three rows and four columns (alternatively, you can think of it as a spreadsheet with sheets, rows, and columns). As you have probably guessed, the reshape function changes the shape of an array. You give it a tuple of integers, corresponding to the new shape. If the dimensions are not compatible with the data, an exception is thrown.

2. We can select a single room by using its three coordinates, namely, the floor, column, and row. For example, the room on the first floor, in the first row, and in the first column (you can have floor 0 and room 0—it's just a matter of convention) can be represented by:

```
In: b[0,0,0]
Out: 0
```

3. If we don't care about the floor, but still want the first column and row, we replace the first index by a : (colon) because we just need to specify the floor number and omit the other indices:

```
In: b[:,0,0]
Out: array([ 0, 12])
This selects the first floor
In: b[0]
Out:
array([[ 0,   1,   2,   3],
       [ 4,   5,   6,   7],
       [ 8,   9,  10,  11]])
```

We could also have written:

```
In: b[0, :, :]
Out:
array([[ 0,   1,   2,   3],
       [ 4,   5,   6,   7],
       [ 8,   9,  10,  11]])
```

An ... (ellipsis) replaces multiple colons, so, the preceding code is equivalent to:

```
In: b[0, ...]
Out:
array([[ 0,   1,   2,   3],
```

```
      [ 4,   5,   6,   7],
      [ 8,   9, 10, 11]])
```

Further, we get the second row on the first floor with:

```
In: b[0,1]
Out: array([4, 5, 6, 7])
```

4. Furthermore, we can also select each second element of this selection:

```
In: b[0,1,::2]
Out: array([4, 6])
```

5. If we want to select all the rooms on both floors that are in the second column, regardless of the row, we will type the following code snippet:

```
In: b[...,1]
Out:
array([[ 1,   5,   9],
       [13, 17, 21]])
```

Similarly, we can select all the rooms on the second row, regardless of floor and column, by writing the following code snippet:

```
In: b[:,1]
Out:
array([[ 4,   5,   6,   7],
       [16, 17, 18, 19]])
```

If we want to select rooms on the ground floor second column, then type the following code snippet:

```
In: b[0,:,1]
Out: array([1, 5, 9])
```

6. If we want to select the first floor, last column, then type the following code snippet:

```
In: b[0,:,-1]
Out: array([ 3,   7, 11])
```

If we want to select rooms on the ground floor, last column reversed, then type the following code snippet:

```
In: b[0,::-1, -1]
Out: array([11,   7,   3])
```

Every second element of that slice:

```
In: b[0,::2,-1]
Out: array([ 3, 11])
```

The command that reverses a one-dimensional array puts the top floor following the ground floor:

```
In: b[::-1]
Out:
array([[[12, 13, 14, 15],
        [16, 17, 18, 19],
        [20, 21, 22, 23]],
       [[ 0,  1,  2,  3],
        [ 4,  5,  6,  7],
        [ 8,  9, 10, 11]]])
```

What just happened?

We sliced a multidimensional NumPy array using several different methods.

Time for action – manipulating array shapes

We already learned about the `reshape` function. Another recurring task is flattening of arrays.

1. **Ravel**: We can accomplish this with the `ravel` function:

```
In: b
Out:
array([[[ 0,  1,  2,  3],
        [ 4,  5,  6,  7],
        [ 8,  9, 10, 11]],
       [[12, 13, 14, 15],
        [16, 17, 18, 19],
        [20, 21, 22, 23]]])
In: b.ravel()
Out:
array([ 0,  1,  2,  3,  4,  5,  6,  7,  8,  9, 10, 11, 12, 13,
14, 15, 16,
       17, 18, 19, 20, 21, 22, 23])
```

2. **Flatten**: The appropriately-named function, `flatten`, does the same as `ravel`, but `flatten` always allocates new memory whereas `ravel` might return a view of the array.

```
In: b.flatten()
Out:
array([ 0,  1,  2,  3,  4,  5,  6,  7,  8,  9, 10, 11, 12, 13,
14, 15, 16,
       17, 18, 19, 20, 21, 22, 23])
```

3. **Setting the shape with a tuple**: Besides the `reshape` function, we can also set the shape directly with a tuple, which is shown as follows:

```
In: b.shape = (6,4)
In: b
Out:
array([[ 0,  1,  2,  3],
       [ 4,  5,  6,  7],
       [ 8,  9, 10, 11],
       [12, 13, 14, 15],
       [16, 17, 18, 19],
       [20, 21, 22, 23]])
```

As you can see, this changes the array directly. Now, we have a six-by-four array.

4. **Transpose**: In linear algebra, it is common to transpose matrices. We can do that too, by using the following code:

```
In: b.transpose()
Out:
array([[ 0,  4,  8, 12, 16, 20],
       [ 1,  5,  9, 13, 17, 21],
       [ 2,  6, 10, 14, 18, 22],
       [ 3,  7, 11, 15, 19, 23]])
```

5. **Resize**: The `resize` method works just like the `reshape` method, but modifies the array it operates on:

```
In: b.resize((2,12))
In: b
Out:
array([[ 0,  1,  2,  3,  4,  5,  6,  7,  8,  9, 10, 11],
       [12, 13, 14, 15, 16, 17, 18, 19, 20, 21, 22, 23]])
```

What just happened?

We manipulated the shapes of NumPy arrays using the `ravel` function, the `flatten` function, the `reshape` function, and the `resize` method.

Stacking

Arrays can be stacked horizontally, depth-wise, or vertically. We can use, for that purpose, the `vstack`, `dstack`, `hstack`, `column_stack`, `row_stack`, and `concatenate` functions.

Time for action – stacking arrays

First, let's set up some arrays:

```
In: a = arange(9).reshape(3,3)
In: a
Out:
array([[0, 1, 2],
       [3, 4, 5],
       [6, 7, 8]])
In: b = 2 * a
In: b
Out:
array([[ 0,  2,  4],
       [ 6,  8, 10],
       [12, 14, 16]])
```

1. **Horizontal stacking**: Starting with horizontal stacking, we will form a tuple of ndarrays and give it to the hstack function. This is shown as follows:

    ```
    In: hstack((a, b))
    Out:
    array([[ 0,  1,  2,  0,  2,  4],
           [ 3,  4,  5,  6,  8, 10],
           [ 6,  7,  8, 12, 14, 16]])
    ```

    We can achieve the same with the concatenate function, which is shown as follows:

    ```
    In: concatenate((a, b), axis=1)
    Out:
    array([[ 0,  1,  2,  0,  2,  4],
           [ 3,  4,  5,  6,  8, 10],
           [ 6,  7,  8, 12, 14, 16]])
    ```

2. **Vertical stacking**: With vertical stacking, again, a tuple is formed. This time, it is given to the `vstack` function. This can be seen as follows:

```
In: vstack((a, b))
Out:
array([[ 0,  1,  2],
       [ 3,  4,  5],
       [ 6,  7,  8],
       [ 0,  2,  4],
       [ 6,  8, 10],
       [12, 14, 16]])
```

The `concatenate` function produces the same result with the axis set to `0`. This is the default value for the axis argument.

```
In: concatenate((a, b), axis=0)
Out:
array([[ 0,  1,  2],
       [ 3,  4,  5],
       [ 6,  7,  8],
       [ 0,  2,  4],
       [ 6,  8, 10],
       [12, 14, 16]])
```

3. **Depth stacking**: Additionally, there is the depth-wise stacking using `dstack` and a tuple, of course. This means stacking of a list of arrays along the third axis (depth). For instance, we could stack 2D arrays of image data on top of each other.

```
In: dstack((a, b))
Out:
array([[[ 0,  0],
        [ 1,  2],
        [ 2,  4]],
       [[ 3,  6],
        [ 4,  8],
        [ 5, 10]],
       [[ 6, 12],
        [ 7, 14],
        [ 8, 16]]])
```

4. **Column stacking**: The `column_stack` function stacks 1D arrays column-wise.
It's shown as follows:

```
In: oned = arange(2)
In: oned
Out: array([0, 1])
In: twice_oned = 2 * oned
In: twice_oned
Out: array([0, 2])
In: column_stack((oned, twice_oned))
Out:
array([[0, 0],
       [1, 2]])
```

2D arrays are stacked the way `hstack` stacks them:

```
In: column_stack((a, b))
Out:
array([[ 0,  1,  2,  0,  2,  4],
       [ 3,  4,  5,  6,  8, 10],
       [ 6,  7,  8, 12, 14, 16]])
In: column_stack((a, b)) == hstack((a, b))
Out:
array([[ True,  True,  True,  True,  True,  True],
       [ True,  True,  True,  True,  True,  True],
       [ True,  True,  True,  True,  True,  True]], dtype=bool)
```

Yes, you guessed it right! We compared two arrays with the `==` operator. Isn't
it beautiful?

5. **Row stacking**: NumPy, of course, also has a function that does row-wise stacking.
It is called `row_stack` and, for 1D arrays, it just stacks the arrays in rows into
a 2D array.

```
In: row_stack((oned, twice_oned))
Out:
array([[0, 1],
       [0, 2]])
```

The `row_stack` function results for 2D arrays are equal to, yes, exactly, the `vstack`
function results.

```
In: row_stack((a, b))
Out:
array([[ 0,  1,  2],
       [ 3,  4,  5],
       [ 6,  7,  8],
```

```
       [ 0,   2,   4],
       [ 6,   8,  10],
       [12,  14,  16]])
In: row_stack((a,b)) == vstack((a, b))
Out:
array([[ True,   True,   True],
       [ True,   True,   True],
       [ True,   True,   True],
       [ True,   True,   True],
       [ True,   True,   True],
       [ True,   True,   True]], dtype=bool)
```

What just happened?

We stacked arrays horizontally, depth-wise, and vertically. We used the `vstack`, `dstack`, `hstack`, `column_stack`, `row_stack`, and `concatenate` functions.

Splitting

Arrays can be split vertically, horizontally, or depth wise. The functions involved are `hsplit`, `vsplit`, `dsplit`, and `split`. We can either split into arrays of the same shape or indicate the position after which the split should occur.

Time for action – splitting arrays

1. **Horizontal splitting**: The ensuing code splits an array along its horizontal axis into three pieces of the same size and shape:

```
In: a
Out:
array([[0, 1, 2],
       [3, 4, 5],
       [6, 7, 8]])
In: hsplit(a, 3)
Out:
[array([[0],
        [3],
        [6]]),
 array([[1],
        [4],
        [7]]),
 array([[2],
        [5],
        [8]])]
```

Compare it with a call of the `split` function, with extra parameter `axis=1`:

```
In: split(a, 3, axis=1)
Out:
[array([[0],
        [3],
        [6]]),
 array([[1],
        [4],
        [7]]),
 array([[2],
        [5],
        [8]])]
```

2. **Vertical splitting**: The `vsplit` function splits along the vertical axis:

```
In: vsplit(a, 3)
Out: [array([[0, 1, 2]]), array([[3, 4, 5]]), array([[6, 7,
8]])]
```

The `split` function, with `axis=0`, also splits along the vertical axis:

```
In: split(a, 3, axis=0)
Out: [array([[0, 1, 2]]), array([[3, 4, 5]]), array([[6, 7,
8]])]
```

3. **Depth-wise splitting**: The `dsplit` function, unsurprisingly, splits depth-wise. We will need an array of rank three first:

```
In: c = arange(27).reshape(3, 3, 3)
In: c
Out:
array([[[ 0,  1,  2],
        [ 3,  4,  5],
        [ 6,  7,  8]],
       [[ 9, 10, 11],
        [12, 13, 14],
        [15, 16, 17]],
       [[18, 19, 20],
        [21, 22, 23],
        [24, 25, 26]]])
In: dsplit(c, 3)
Out:
[array([[[ 0],
        [ 3],
        [ 6]],
       [[ 9],
```

```
       [12],
       [15]],
      [[18],
       [21],
       [24]]]),
array([[[ 1],
        [ 4],
        [ 7]],
       [[10],
        [13],
        [16]],
       [[19],
        [22],
        [25]]]),
array([[[ 2],
        [ 5],
        [ 8]],
       [[11],
        [14],
        [17]],
       [[20],
        [23],
        [26]]])]
```

What just happened?

We split arrays using the `hsplit`, `vsplit`, `dsplit`, and `split` functions.

Array attributes

Besides the `shape` and `dtype` attributes, `ndarray` has a number of other attributes, as shown in the following list:

- ◆ The `ndim` attribute gives the number of dimensions:

```
In: b
Out:
array([[ 0,  1,  2,  3,  4,  5,  6,  7,  8,  9, 10, 11],
       [12, 13, 14, 15, 16, 17, 18, 19, 20, 21, 22, 23]])
In: b.ndim
Out: 2
```

◆ The `size` attribute contains the number of elements. This is shown a follows:

```
In: b.size
Out: 24
```

◆ The `itemsize` attribute gives the number of bytes for each element in the array:

```
In: b.itemsize
Out: 8
```

◆ If you want the total number of bytes the array requires, you can have a look at `nbytes`. This is just a product of the `itemsize` and `size` attributes:

```
In: b.nbytes
Out: 192
In: b.size * b.itemsize
Out: 192
```

◆ The `T` attribute has the same effect as the `transpose` function, which is shown as follows:

```
In: b.resize(6,4)
In: b
Out:
array([[ 0,  1,  2,  3],
       [ 4,  5,  6,  7],
       [ 8,  9, 10, 11],
       [12, 13, 14, 15],
       [16, 17, 18, 19],
       [20, 21, 22, 23]])
In: b.T
Out:
array([[ 0,  4,  8, 12, 16, 20],
       [ 1,  5,  9, 13, 17, 21],
       [ 2,  6, 10, 14, 18, 22],
       [ 3,  7, 11, 15, 19, 23]])
```

◆ If the array has a rank lower than two, we will just get a view of the array:

```
In: b.ndim
Out: 1
In: b.T
Out: array([0, 1, 2, 3, 4])
```

◆ Complex numbers in NumPy are represented by `j`. For example, we can create an array with complex numbers:

```
In: b = array([1.j + 1, 2.j + 3])
In: b
Out: array([ 1.+1.j,  3.+2.j])
```

◆ The `real` attribute gives us the real part of the array, or the array itself if it only contains real numbers:

```
In: b.real
Out: array([ 1.,   3.])
```

◆ The `imag` attribute contains the imaginary part of the array:

```
In: b.imag
Out: array([ 1.,   2.])
```

◆ If the array contains complex numbers, then the data type is automatically also complex:

```
In: b.dtype
Out: dtype('complex128')
In: b.dtype.str
Out: '<c16'
```

◆ The `flat` attribute returns a `numpy.flatiter` object. This is the only way to acquire a `flatiter`—we do not have access to a `flatiter` constructor. The flat iterator enables us to loop through an array as if it is a flat array, as shown next:

```
In: b = arange(4).reshape(2,2)
In: b
Out:
array([[0, 1],
       [2, 3]])
In: f = b.flat
In: f
Out: <numpy.flatiter object at 0x103013e00>
In: for item in f: print item
   .....:
0
1
2
3
```

It is possible to directly get an element with the `flatiter` object:

```
In: b.flat[2]
Out: 2
```

Or multiple elements:

```
In: b.flat[[1,3]]
Out: array([1, 3])
```

The `flat` attribute is settable. Setting the value of the `flat` attribute leads to overwriting the values of the whole array:

```
In: b.flat = 7
In: b
Out:
array([[7, 7],
       [7, 7]])
or selected elements
In: b.flat[[1,3]] = 1
In: b
Out:
array([[7, 1],
       [7, 1]])
```

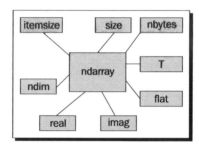

Time for action – converting arrays

We can convert a NumPy array to a Python list with the `tolist` function:

1. **Convert to a list:**

```
In: b
Out: array([ 1.+1.j,  3.+2.j])
In: b.tolist()
Out: [(1+1j), (3+2j)]
```

2. The `astype` function converts the array to an array of the specified type:

```
In: b
Out: array([ 1.+1.j,  3.+2.j])
In: b.astype(int)
/usr/local/bin/ipython:1: ComplexWarning: Casting complex values
to real discards the imaginary part
  #!/usr/bin/python
Out: array([1, 3])
```

We are losing the imaginary part when casting from complex type to `int`.
The `astype` function also accepts the name of a type as a string.

```
In: b.astype('complex')
Out: array([ 1.+1.j,  3.+2.j])
```

It won't show any warning this time, because we used the proper data type.

What just happened?

We converted NumPy arrays to a list and to arrays of different data types.

Summary

We learned a lot in this chapter about the NumPy fundamentals: data types and arrays. Arrays have several attributes describing them. We learned that one of these attributes is the data type, which in NumPy, is represented by a full-fledged object.

NumPy arrays can be sliced and indexed in an efficient manner, just like Python lists. NumPy arrays have the added ability of working with multiple dimensions.

The shape of an array can be manipulated in many ways—stacking, resizing, reshaping, and splitting. A great number of convenience functions for shape manipulation were demonstrated in this chapter.

Having learned about the basics, it's time to move on to the study of commonly-used functions in *Chapter 3, Get to Terms with Commonly Used Functions*. This includes basic statistical and mathematical functions.

3

Get in Terms with Commonly Used Functions

In this chapter, we will have a look at common NumPy functions. In particular, we will learn how to load data from files using a historical stock prices example. Also, we will get to see the basic NumPy mathematical and statistical functions. We will learn how to read from and write to files. Also, we will get a taste of the functional programming and linear algebra possibilities in NumPy.

In this chapter, we shall cover the following topics:

- ◆ Functions working on arrays
- ◆ Loading arrays from files
- ◆ Writing arrays to files
- ◆ Simple mathematical and statistical functions

File I/O

First, we will learn about file I/O with NumPy. Data is usually stored in files. You will not get far if you are not able to read from and write to files.

Time for action – reading and writing files

As an example of file I/O, we will create an identity matrix and store its contents in a file.
Perform the following steps to do so:

1. The identity matrix is a square matrix with ones on the main diagonal and zeroes
for the rest. The identity matrix can be created with the `eye` function. The only
argument we need to give the `eye` function is the number of ones. So, for instance,
for a 2 x 2 matrix, write the following code:

```
i2 = np.eye(2)
print i2
The output is:
[[ 1.   0.]
 [ 0.   1.]]
```

2. Save the data using the `savetxt` function. We obviously need to specify the name
of the file that we want to save the data in and the array containing the data itself.

```
np.savetxt("eye.txt", i2)
```

A file called `eye.txt` should have been created. You can check for yourself whether the
contents are as expected. The code for this example can be downloaded from the book
support website `http://www.packtpub.com/support` (see `save.py`).

```
import numpy as np

i2 = np.eye(2)
print i2
np.savetxt("eye.txt", i2)
```

What just happened?

Reading and writing files is a necessary skill for data analysis. We wrote to a file using
`savetxt`. We made an identity matrix with the `eye` function.

CSV files

Files in the **comma-separated values (CSV)** format are encountered quite frequently. Often,
the CSV file is just a dump from a database file. Usually, each field in the CSV file corresponds
to a database table column. As we all know, spreadsheet programs, such as Excel, can
produce CSV files as well.

Time for action – loading from CSV files

How do we deal with CSV files? Luckily, the `loadtxt` function can conveniently read CSV files, split up the fields, and load the data into NumPy arrays. In the following example, we will load historical price data for Apple (the company, not the fruit). The data is in the CSV format. The first column contains a symbol that identifies the stock. In our case, it is `AAPL`. Second is the date in the *dd-mm-yyyy* format. The third column is empty. Then, in order, we have the open, high, low, and close price. Last, but not least, is the volume of the day. This is what a line looks like:

```
AAPL,28-01-2011, ,344.17,344.4,333.53,336.1,21144800
```

For now, we are only interested in the close price and volume. In the preceding sample, that would be `336.1` and `21144800`. Store the close price and volume in two arrays, as follows:

```
c,v=np.loadtxt('data.csv', delimiter=',', usecols=(6,7), unpack=True)
```

As you can see, data is stored in the `data.csv` file. We have set the delimiter to `','` (comma), since we are dealing with a comma-separated value file. The `usecols` parameter is set through a tuple to get the seventh and eighth fields, which correspond to the close price and volume. `unpack` is set to `True`, which means that data will be unpacked and assigned to the `c` and `v` variables that will hold the close price and volume, respectively.

What just happened?

CSV files are a special type of file that we have to deal with frequently. We read a CSV file containing stock quotes with the `loadtxt` function. We indicated to the `loadtxt` function that the delimiter of our file was a comma. We specified which columns we were interested in, through the `usecols` argument, and set the `unpack` parameter to `True` so that the data was unpacked for further use.

Volume-weighted average price

Volume-weighted average price (VWAP) is a very important quantity in finance. It represents an "average" price for a financial asset. The higher the volume, the more significant a price move typically is. VWAP is often used in algorithmic trading and is calculated by using volume values as weights.

Time for action – calculating volume-weighted average price

The following are the actions that we will take:

1. Read the data into arrays.

2. Calculate VWAP.

```
import numpy as np
c,v=np.loadtxt('data.csv', delimiter=',', usecols=(6,7),
unpack=True)
vwap = np.average(c, weights=v)
print "VWAP =", vwap
The output is
VWAP = 350.589549353
```

What just happened?

That wasn't very hard, was it? We just called the `average` function and set its `weights` parameter to use the `v` array for weights. By the way, NumPy also has a function to calculate the arithmetic mean.

The mean function

The `mean` function is quite friendly and not so mean. This function calculates the arithmetic mean of an array. Let's see it in action:

```
print "mean =", np.mean(c)
mean =   351.037666667
```

Time-weighted average price

In finance, TWAP is another "average" price measure. Now that we are at it, let's compute the time-weighted average price, too. It is just a variation on a theme really. The idea is that recent price quotes are more important, so we should give recent prices higher weights. The easiest way is to create an array with the `arange` function of increasing values from zero to the number of elements in the close price array. This is not necessarily the correct way. In fact, most of the examples concerning stock price analysis in this book are only illustrative. The following is the TWAP code:

```
t = np.arange(len(c))
print "twap =", np.average(c, weights=t)
```

It produces the following output:

```
twap = 352.428321839
```

The TWAP is even higher than the mean.

Pop quiz – computing the weighted average

Q1. Which function returns the weighted average of an array?

1. `weighted average`

2. `waverage`

3. `average`

4. `avg`

Have a go hero – calculating other averages

Try doing the same calculation using the open price. Calculate the mean for the volume and the other prices.

Value range

Usually, we don't only want to know the average or arithmetic mean of a set of values, which are sort of in the middle; we also want the extremes, the full range—the highest and lowest values. The sample data that we are using here already has those values per day—the high and low price. However, we need to know the highest value of the high price and the lowest price value of the low price. After all, how else would we know how much our Apple stocks would gain or lose?

Time for action – finding highest and lowest values

The `min` and `max` functions are the answer to our requirement. Perform the following steps to find highest and lowest values:

1. First, we will need to read our file again and store the values for the high and low prices into arrays.

   ```
   h,l=np.loadtxt('data.csv', delimiter=',', usecols=(4,5),
   unpack=True)
   ```

   The only thing that changed is the `usecols` parameter, since the high and low prices are situated in different columns.

2. The following code gets the price range:

   ```
   print "highest =", np.max(h)
   print "lowest =", np.min(l)
   ```

These are the values returned:

```
highest = 364.9
lowest = 333.53
```

Now, it's trivial to get a midpoint, so it is left as an exercise for the reader to attempt.

3. NumPy allows us to compute the spread of an array with a function called `ptp`. The `ptp` function returns the difference between the maximum and minimum values of an array. In other words, it is equal to *max(array) - min(array)*. Call the `ptp` function.

```
print "Spread high price", np.ptp(h)
print "Spread low price", np.ptp(l)
```

You will see the following:

```
Spread high price 24.86
Spread low price 26.97
```

What just happened?

We defined a range of highest to lowest values for the price. The highest value was given by applying the `max` function to the high price array. Similarly, the lowest value was found by calling the `min` function to the low price array. We also calculated the peak-to-peak distance with the `ptp` function.

```
import numpy as np

h,l=np.loadtxt('data.csv', delimiter=',', usecols=(4,5), unpack=True)
print "highest =", np.max(h)
print "lowest =", np.min(l)
print (np.max(h) + np.min(l)) /2

print "Spread high price", np.ptp(h)
print "Spread low price", np.ptp(l)
```

Statistics

Stock traders are interested in the most probable close price. Common sense says that this should be close to some kind of an average. The arithmetic mean and weighted average are ways to find the center of a distribution of values. However, neither are robust nor sensitive to outliers. For instance, if we had a close price value of a million dollars, this would have influenced the outcome of our calculations.

Time for action – doing simple statistics

We can use some kind of threshold to weed out outliers, but there is a better way. It is called the median, and it basically picks the middle value of a sorted set of values. For example, if we have the values of 1, 2, 3, 4, and 5, the median would be 3, since it is in the middle. The following are the steps to calculate the median:

1. Determine the median of the close price. Create a new Python script and call it `simplestats.py`. You already know how to load the data from a CSV file into an array. So, copy that line of code and make sure that it only gets the close price. The code should appear like the following, by now:

    ```
    c=np.loadtxt('data.csv', delimiter=',', usecols=(6,), unpack=True)
    ```

2. The function that will do the magic for us is called median. We will call it and print the result immediately. Add the following line of code:

    ```
    print "median =", np.median(c)
    ```

    The program prints the following output:

    ```
    median = 352.055
    ```

3. Since it is our first time using the median function, we would like to check whether this is correct. Not because we are paranoid or anything! Obviously, we could do it by just going through the file and finding the correct value, but that is no fun. Instead, we will just mimic the median algorithm by sorting the close price array and printing the middle value of the sorted array. The `msort` function does the first part for us. We will call the function, store the sorted array, and then print it.

    ```
    sorted_close = np.msort(c)
    print "sorted =", sorted_close
    ```

    This prints the following output:

    ```
    sorted = [ 336.1    338.61  339.32  342.62  342.88  343.44  344.32  345.03  346.5
      346.67  348.16  349.31  350.56  351.88  351.99  352.12  352.47  353.21
      354.54  355.2   355.36  355.76  356.85  358.16  358.3   359.18  359.56
      359.9   360.    363.13]
    ```

    Yup, it works! Let's now get the middle value of the sorted array:

    ```
    N = len(c)
    print "middle =", sorted[(N - 1)/2]
    ```

    It gives us the following output:

    ```
    middle = 351.99
    ```

4. Hey, that's a different value than the one the `median` function gave us. How come? Upon further investigation we find that the `median` function return value doesn't even appear in our file. That's even stranger! Before filing bugs with the NumPy team, let's have a look at the documentation. This mystery is easy to solve. It turns out that our naive algorithm only works for arrays with odd lengths. For even-length arrays, the median is calculated from the average of the two array values in the middle. Therefore, type the following code:

```
print "average middle =", (sorted[N /2] + sorted[(N - 1) / 2]) / 2
```

This prints the following output:

```
average middle = 352.055
```

Success!

5. Another statistical measure that we are concerned with is variance. Variance tells us how much a variable varies. In our case, it also tells us how risky an investment is, since a stock price that varies too wildly is bound to get us into trouble. With NumPy, this is just a one liner. See the following code:

```
print "variance =", np.var(c)
```

This gives us the following output:

```
variance = 50.1265178889
```

6. Not that we don't trust NumPy or anything, but let's double-check using the definition of variance, as found in the documentation. Mind you, this definition might be different than the one in your statistics book, but that is quite common in the field of statistics.

 The **variance** is defined as the mean of the square of deviations from the mean, divided by the number of elements in the array.

Some books tell us to divide by the number of elements in the array minus one.

```
print "variance from definition =", np.mean((c - c.mean())**2)
```

The output is as follows:

```
variance from definition = 50.1265178889
```

Just as we expected!

What just happened?

Maybe you noticed something new. We suddenly called the `mean` function on the `c` array. Yes, this is legal, because the `ndarray` object has a `mean` method. This is for your convenience. For now, just keep in mind that this is possible. The code for this example can be found in `simplestats.py`.

```
import numpy as np

c=np.loadtxt('data.csv', delimiter=',', usecols=(6,), unpack=True)
print "median =", np.median(c)
sorted = np.msort(c)
print "sorted =", sorted

N = len(c)
print "middle =", sorted[(N - 1)/2]
print "average middle =", (sorted[N /2] + sorted[(N - 1) / 2]) / 2

print "variance =", np.var(c)
print "variance from definition =", np.mean((c - c.mean())**2)
```

Stock returns

In academic literature it is more common to base analysis on stock returns and log returns of the close price. Simple returns are just the rate of change from one value to the next. Logarithmic returns or log returns are determined by taking the log of all the prices and calculating the differences between them. In high school, we learned that the difference between the log of "a" and the log of "b" is equal to the log of "a divided by b". Log returns, therefore, also measure rate of change. Returns are dimensionless, since, in the act of dividing, we divide dollar by dollar (or some other currency). Anyway, investors are most likely to be interested in the variance or standard deviation of the returns, as this represents risk.

Time for action – analyzing stock returns

Perform the following steps to analyze stock returns:

1. First, let's calculate simple returns. NumPy has the `diff` function that returns an array built up of the difference between two consecutive array elements. This is sort of like differentiation in calculus. To get the returns, we also have to divide by the value of the previous day. We must be careful though. The array returned by `diff` is one element shorter than the close prices array. After careful deliberation, we get the following code:

```
returns = np.diff( arr ) / arr[ : -1]
```

Notice that we don't use the last value in the divisor. Let's compute the standard deviation using the `std` function:

```
print "Standard deviation =", np.std(returns)
```

This results in the following output:

```
Standard deviation = 0.0129221344368
```

2. The log return is even easier to calculate. We use the `log` function to get the log of the close price and then unleash the `diff` function on the result.

```
logreturns = np.diff( np.log(c) )
```

Normally, we would have to check that the input array doesn't have zeroes or negative numbers. If it did, we would have got an error. Stock prices are, however, always positive, so we didn't have to check.

3. Quite likely, we will be interested in days when the return is positive. In the current setup, we can get the next best thing with the `where` function, which returns the indices of an array that satisfies a condition. Just type the following code:

```
posretindices = np.where(returns > 0)
print "Indices with positive returns", posretindices
```

This gives us a number of indices for the array elements that are positive.

```
Indices with positive returns (array([ 0,  1,  4,  5,  6,  7,  9,
10, 11, 12, 16, 17, 18, 19, 21, 22, 23, 25, 28]),)
```

4. In investing, volatility measures price variation of a financial security. Historical volatility is calculated from historical price data. The logarithmic returns are interesting if you want to know the historical volatility—for instance, the annualized or monthly volatility. The annualized volatility is equal to the standard deviation of the log returns as a ratio of its mean, divided by one over the square root of the number of business days in a year, usually one assumes 252. Calculate it with the `std` and mean functions. See the following code:

```
annual_volatility = np.std(logreturns)/np.mean(logreturns)
annual_volatility = annual_volatility / np.sqrt(1./252.)
print annual_volatility
```

5. Take note of the division within the `sqrt` function. Since, in Python, integer division works differently than float division, we needed to use floats to make sure that we get the proper results. Similarly, the monthly volatility is given by:

```
print "Monthly volatility", annual_volatility * np.sqrt(1./12.)
```

What just happened?

We calculated the simple stock returns with the `diff` function, which calculates differences between sequential elements. The `log` function computes the natural logarithms of array elements. We used it to calculate the logarithmic returns. At the end of the tutorial we calculated the annual and monthly volatility (see `returns.py`).

```
import numpy as np

c=np.loadtxt('data.csv', delimiter=',', usecols=(6,), unpack=True)

returns = np.diff( c ) / c[ : -1]
print "Standard deviation =", np.std(returns)

logreturns = np.diff( np.log(c) )

posretindices = np.where(returns > 0)
print "Indices with positive returns", posretindices

annual_volatility = np.std(logreturns)/np.mean(logreturns)
annual_volatility = annual_volatility / np.sqrt(1./252.)
print "Annual volatility", annual_volatility

print "Monthly volatility", annual_volatility * np.sqrt(1./12.)
```

Dates

Do you sometimes have the Monday blues or the Friday fever? Ever wondered whether the stock market suffers from said phenomena? Well, I think this certainly warrants extensive research.

Time for action – dealing with dates

First, we will read the close price data. Second, we will split the prices according to the day of the week. Third, for each weekday, we will calculate the average price. Finally, we will find out which day of the week has the highest average and which has the lowest average. A health warning before we commence – you might be tempted to use the result to buy stock on one day and sell on the other. However, we don't have enough data to make this kind of decision. Please consult a professional statistician first!

Coders hate dates because they are so complicated! NumPy is very much oriented towards floating point operations. For that reason, we need to take extra effort to process dates. Try it out yourself; put the following code in a script or use the one that comes with the book:

```
dates, close=np.loadtxt('data.csv', delimiter=',',
    usecols=(1,6), unpack=True)
```

Execute the script and the following error will appear:

```
ValueError: invalid literal for float(): 28-01-2011
```

Now perform the following steps to deal with dates:

1. Obviously, NumPy tried to convert the dates into floats. What we have to do is explicitly tell NumPy how to convert the dates. The `loadtxt` function has a special parameter for this purpose. The parameter is called `converters` and is a dictionary that links columns with so-called converter functions. It is our responsibility to write the converter function.

    Let's write the function down:

    ```
    # Monday 0
    # Tuesday 1
    # Wednesday 2
    # Thursday 3
    # Friday 4
    # Saturday 5
    # Sunday 6
    def datestr2num(s):
        return datetime.datetime.strptime
        (s, "%d-%m-%Y").date().weekday()
    ```

    We give the `datestr2num` function dates as a string, such as "28-01-2011". The string is first turned into a `datetime` object using a specified format `"%d-%m-%Y"`. This is, by the way, standard Python and is not related to NumPy itself. Second, the `datetime` object is turned into a day. Finally the `weekday` method is called on the date to return a number. As you can read in the comments, the number is between 0 and 6. 0 is for instance Monday and 6 is Sunday. The actual number, of course, is not important for our algorithm; it is only used as identification.

2. Now we will hook up our date converter function to load the data.

    ```
    dates, close=np.loadtxt('data.csv', delimiter=',', usecols=(1,6),
    converters={1: datestr2num}, unpack=True)
    print "Dates =", dates
    ```

This prints the following output:

```
Dates = [ 4.  0.  1.  2.  3.  4.  0.  1.  2.  3.  4.  0.  1.  2.
3.  4.  1.  2.  4.  0.  1.  2.  3.  4.  0.  1.  2.  3.  4.]
```

No Saturdays and Sundays, as you can see. Exchanges are closed over the weekend.

3. We will now make an array that has five elements for each day of the week. The values of the array will be initialized to 0.

```
averages = np.zeros(5)
```

This array will hold the averages for each weekday.

4. We already learned about the `where` function that returns indices of the array for elements that conform to a specified condition. The `take` function can use these indices and takes the values of the corresponding array items. We will use the `take` function to get the close prices for each weekday. In the following loop we go through the date values 0 to 4, better known as Monday to Friday. We get the indices with the `where` function for each day and store it in the `indices` array. Then, we retrieve the values corresponding to the indices, using the `take` function. Finally, we compute an average for each weekday and store it in the `averages` array, as follows:

```
for i in range(5):
    indices = np.where(dates == i)
    prices = np.take(close, indices)
    avg = np.mean(prices)
    print "Day", i, "prices", prices, "Average", avg
    averages[i] = avg
```

The loop prints the following output:

```
Day 0 prices [[ 339.32  351.88  359.18  353.21  355.36]] Average
351.79
Day 1 prices [[ 345.03  355.2   359.9   338.61  349.31  355.76]]
Average 350.635
Day 2 prices [[ 344.32  358.16  363.13  342.62  352.12  352.47]]
Average 352.136666667
Day 3 prices [[ 343.44  354.54  358.3   342.88  359.56  346.67]]
Average 350.898333333
Day 4 prices [[ 336.1   346.5   356.85  350.56  348.16  360.
351.99]] Average 350.022857143
```

5. If you want, you can go ahead and find out which day has the highest, and which the lowest, average. However, it is just as easy to find this out with the `max` and `min` functions, as shown next:

```
top = np.max(averages)
print "Highest average", top
print "Top day of the week",  np.argmax(averages)
bottom = np.min(averages)
print "Lowest average", bottom
print "Bottom day of the week",  np.argmin(averages)
```

The output is as follows:

```
Highest average 352.136666667
Top day of the week 2
Lowest average 350.022857143
Bottom day of the week 4
```

What just happened?

The `argmin` function returned the index of the lowest value in the `averages` array. The index returned was 4, which corresponds to Friday. The `argmax` function returned the index of the highest value in the `averages` array. The index returned was 2, which corresponds to Wednesday (see `weekdays.py`).

```
import numpy as np
from datetime import datetime

# Monday 0
# Tuesday 1
# Wednesday 2
# Thursday 3
# Friday 4
# Saturday 5
# Sunday 6
def datestr2num(s):
    return datetime.strptime(s, "%d-%m-%Y").date().weekday()

dates, close=np.loadtxt('data.csv', delimiter=',', usecols=(1,6),
converters={1: datestr2num}, unpack=True)
print "Dates =", dates

averages = np.zeros(5)

for i in range(5):
    indices = np.where(dates == i)
    prices = np.take(close, indices)
    avg = np.mean(prices)
```

```
    print "Day", i, "prices", prices, "Average", avg
    averages[i] = avg


top = np.max(averages)
print "Highest average", top
print "Top day of the week", np.argmax(averages)

bottom = np.min(averages)
print "Lowest average", bottom
print "Bottom day of the week", np.argmin(averages
```

Have a go hero – looking at VWAP and TWAP

Hey, that was fun! For the sample data, it appears that Friday is the cheapest day and Wednesday is the day when your Apple stock will be worth the most. Ignoring the fact that we have very little data, is there a better method to compute the averages? Shouldn't we involve volume data as well? Maybe it makes more sense to you to do a time-weighted average. Give it a go! Calculate the VWAP and TWAP. You can find some hints on how to go about doing this at the beginning of this chapter.

Weekly summary

The data that we used in the previous *Time for action* tutorials is end-of-day data. In essence, it is summarized data compiled from trade data for a certain day. If you are interested in the cotton market and have decades of data, you might want to summarize and compress the data even further. Let's do that. Let's summarize the data of Apple stocks to give us weekly summaries.

Time for action – summarizing data

The data we will summarize will be for a whole business week from Monday to Friday. During the period covered by the data, there was one holiday on February 21st, President's Day. This happened to be a Monday and the US stock exchanges were closed on this day. As a consequence, there is no entry for this day, in the sample. The first day in the sample is a Friday, which is inconvenient. Use the following instructions to summarize data:

1. To simplify, we will just have a look at the first three weeks in the sample—you can later have a go at improving this.

    ```
    close = close[:16]
    dates = dates[:16]
    ```

    We will build on the code from the *Time for action – dealing with dates* tutorial.

2. Commencing, we will find the first Monday in our sample data. Recall that Mondays have the code 0 in Python. This is what we will put in the condition of a `where` function. Then, we will need to extract the first element that has index 0. The result would be a multidimensional array. Flatten that with the `ravel` function.

```
# get first Monday
first_monday = np.ravel(np.where(dates == 0))[0]
print "The first Monday index is", first_monday
```

This will print the following output:

```
The first Monday index is 1
```

3. The next logical step is to find the Friday before last Friday in the sample. The logic is similar to the one for finding the first Monday, and the code for Friday is 4. Additionally, we are looking for the second-to-last element with index 2.

```
# get last Friday
last_friday = np.ravel(np.where(dates == 4))[-2]
print "The last Friday index is", last_friday
```

This will give us the following output:

```
The last Friday index is 15
```

Next, create an array with the indices of all the days in the three weeks:

```
weeks_indices = np.arange(first_monday, last_friday + 1)
print "Weeks indices initial", weeks_indices
```

4. Split the array in pieces of size 5 with the `split` function.

```
weeks_indices = np.split(weeks_indices, 5)
print "Weeks indices after split", weeks_indices
```

It splits the array, as follows:

```
Weeks indices after split [array([1, 2, 3, 4, 5]), array([ 6,   7,
8,   9, 10]), array([11, 12, 13, 14, 15])]
```

5. In NumPy, dimensions are called axes. Now, we will get fancy with the `apply_along_axis` function. This function calls another function, which we will provide, to operate on each of the elements of an array. Currently, we have an array with three elements. Each array item corresponds to one week in our sample and contains indices of the corresponding items. Call the `apply_along_axis` function by supplying the name of our function, called `summarize`, that we will define shortly. Further specify the axis or dimension number (such as 1), the array to operate on, and a variable number of arguments for the `summarize` function, if any.

```
weeksummary = np.apply_along_axis(summarize, 1, weeks_indices,
open, high, low, close)
print "Week summary", weeksummary
```

6. Write the `summarize` function. The `summarize` function returns, for each week, a tuple that holds the open, high, low, and close prices for the week, similarly to end-of-day data.

```
def summarize(a, o, h, l, c):
    monday_open = o[a[0]]
    week_high = np.max( np.take(h, a) )
    week_low = np.min( np.take(l, a) )
    friday_close = c[a[-1]]


    return("APPL", monday_open, week_high, week_low, friday_close)
```

Notice that we used the `take` function to get the actual values from indices. Calculating the high and low values of the week was easily done with the `max` and `min` functions. `open` for the week is the open for the first day in the week—Monday. Likewise, `close` is the close for the last day of the week—Friday.

```
Week summary [['APPL' '335.8' '346.7' '334.3' '346.5']
 ['APPL' '347.89' '360.0' '347.64' '356.85']
 ['APPL' '356.79' '364.9' '349.52' '350.56']]
```

7. Store the data in a file with the NumPy `savetxt` function.

```
np.savetxt("weeksummary.csv", weeksummary, delimiter=",",
fmt="%s")
```

As you can see, we specify a filename, the array we want to store, a delimiter (in this case a comma), and the format we want to store floating point numbers in.

The format string starts with a percent sign. Second is an optional flag. The - flag means left justify, 0 means left pad with zeroes, + means precede with + or -. Third is an optional width. The width indicates the minimum number of characters. Fourth, a dot is followed by a number linked to precision. Finally, there comes a character specifier; in our example, the character specifier is a string.

Character code	Description
c	character
d or i	signed decimal integer
e or E	scientific notation with e or E
f	decimal floating point
g or G	use the shorter of e, E, or f
o	signed octal

Character code	Description
s	string of characters
u	unsigned decimal integer
x or X	unsigned hexadecimal integer

View the generated file in your favorite editor or type in the following commands in the command line:

```
cat weeksummary.csv
APPL,335.8,346.7,334.3,346.5
APPL,347.89,360.0,347.64,356.85
APPL,356.79,364.9,349.52,350.56
```

What just happened?

We did something that is not even possible in some programming languages. We defined a function and passed it as an argument to the apply_along_axis function. Arguments for the summarize function were neatly passed by apply_along_axis (see weeksummary.py).

```
import numpy as np
from datetime import datetime

# Monday 0
# Tuesday 1
# Wednesday 2
# Thursday 3
# Friday 4
# Saturday 5
# Sunday 6
def datestr2num(s):
    return datetime.strptime(s, "%d-%m-%Y").date().weekday()

dates, open, high, low, close=np.loadtxt('data.csv', delimiter=',',
usecols=(1, 3, 4, 5, 6), converters={1: datestr2num}, unpack=True)
close = close[:16]
dates = dates[:16]

# get first Monday
first_monday = np.ravel(np.where(dates == 0))[0]
print "The first Monday index is", first_monday

# get last Friday
```

```
last_friday = np.ravel(np.where(dates == 4))[-1]
print "The last Friday index is", last_friday

weeks_indices = np.arange(first_monday, last_friday + 1)
print "Weeks indices initial", weeks_indices

weeks_indices = np.split(weeks_indices, 3)
print "Weeks indices after split", weeks_indices

def summarize(a, o, h, l, c):
    monday_open = o[a[0]]
    week_high = np.max( np.take(h, a) )
    week_low = np.min( np.take(l, a) )
    friday_close = c[a[-1]]

    return("APPL", monday_open, week_high, week_low, friday_close)

weeksummary = np.apply_along_axis(summarize, 1, weeks_indices, open,
high, low, close)
print "Week summary", weeksummary

np.savetxt("weeksummary.csv", weeksummary, delimiter=",", fmt="%s")
```

Have a go hero – improving the code

Change the code to deal with a holiday. Time the code to see how big the speedup due to `apply_along_axis` is.

Average true range

The **average true range (ATR)** is a technical indicator that measures volatility of stock prices. The ATR calculation is not important further but will serve as an example of several NumPy functions, including the `maximum` function.

Time for action – calculating the average true range

To calculate the average true range, perform the following steps:

1. The ATR is based on the low and high price of *N* days, usually the last 20 days.

```
N = int(sys.argv[1])
h = h[-N:]
l = l[-N:]
```

2. We also need to know the close price of the previous day.

```
previousclose = c[-N -1: -1]
```

For each day, we calculate the following:

- ❑ `h - l`: The daily range (the difference between high and low price)

- ❑ `h - previousclose`: The difference between high price and previous close

- ❑ `previousclose - l`: The difference between the previous close and the low price

3. The `max` function returns the maximum of an array. Based on those three values, we calculate the so-called true range, which is the maximum of these values. We are now interested in the element-wise maxima across arrays—meaning the maxima of the first elements in the arrays, the second elements in the arrays, and so on. Use the NumPy `maximum` function instead of the `max` function for this purpose.

```
truerange = np.maximum(h - l, h - previousclose, previousclose - l)
```

4. Create an `atr` array of size `N` and initialize its values to 0.

```
atr = np.zeros(N)
```

5. The first value of the array is just the average of the `truerange` array.

```
atr[0] = np.mean(truerange)
```

Calculate the other values with the following formula:

$$\frac{((N-1)PATR+TR)}{N}$$

Here, PATR is the previous day's ATR; TR is the true range.

```
for i in range(1, N):
    atr[i] = (N - 1) * atr[i - 1] + truerange[i]
    atr[i] /= N
```

What just happened?

We formed three arrays, one for each of the three ranges—daily range, the gap between the high of today and the close of yesterday, and the gap between the close of yesterday and the low of today. This tells us how much the stock price moved and, therefore, how volatile it is. The algorithm requires us to find the maximum value for each day. The `max` function that we used before can give us the maximum value within an array, but that is not what we want here. We need the maximum value across arrays, so we want the maximum value of the first elements in the three arrays, the second elements, and so on. In this *Time for action* tutorial, we saw that the `maximum` function can do this. After that, we computed a moving average of the true range values (see `atr.py`).

```python
import numpy as np
import sys

h, l, c = np.loadtxt('data.csv', delimiter=',', usecols=(4, 5, 6),
unpack=True)

N = int(sys.argv[1])
h = h[-N:]
l = l[-N:]

print "len(h)", len(h), "len(l)", len(l)
print "Close", c
previousclose = c[-N -1: -1]

print "len(previousclose)", len(previousclose)
print "Previous close", previousclose
truerange = np.maximum(h - l, h - previousclose, previousclose - l)

print "True range", truerange

atr = np.zeros(N)

atr[0] = np.mean(truerange)

for i in range(1, N):
    atr[i] = (N - 1) * atr[i - 1] + truerange[i]
    atr[i] /= N

print "ATR", atr
```

In the following tutorials, we will learn better ways to calculate moving averages.

Have a go hero – taking the minimum function for a spin

Besides the `maximum` function, there is a `minimum` function. You can probably guess what it does. Make a small script or start an interactive session in IPython to prove your assumptions.

Simple moving average

The simple moving average is commonly used to analyze time-series data. To calculate it, we define a moving window of *N* periods, *N* days in our case. We move this window along the data and calculate the mean of the values inside the window.

Time for action – computing the simple moving average

The moving average is easy enough to compute with a few loops and the mean function, but NumPy has a better alternative—the `convolve` function. The simple moving average is, after all, nothing more than a convolution with equal weights or, if you like, unweighted.

 Convolution is a mathematical operation on two functions defined as the integral of the product of the two functions after one of the functions is reversed and shifted.

Use the following steps to compute the simple moving average:

1. Use the `ones` function to create an array of size N and elements initialized to 1; then, divide the array by N to give us the weights, as follows:

```
N = int(sys.argv[1])
weights = np.ones(N) / N
print "Weights", weights
```

For N = 5, this code gives us the following output:

```
Weights [ 0.2  0.2  0.2  0.2  0.2]
```

2. Now call the `convolve` function with the following weights:

```
c = np.loadtxt('data.csv', delimiter=',', usecols=(6,),
unpack=True)
sma = np.convolve(weights, c)[N-1:-N+1]]
```

3. From the array returned by `convolve`, we extracted the data in the center of size N. The following code makes an array of time values and plots with `Matplotlib` that we will be covering in a later chapter.

```
c = np.loadtxt('data.csv', delimiter=',', usecols=(6,),
unpack=True)
sma = np.convolve(weights, c)[N-1:-N+1]
t = np.arange(N - 1, len(c))
plot(t, c[N-1:], lw=1.0)
plot(t, sma, lw=2.0)
show()
```

In the following chart, the smooth thick line is the 5-day simple moving average and the jagged thin line is the close price:

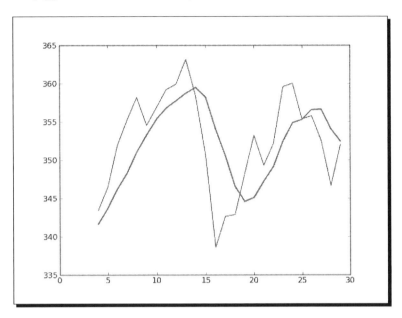

What just happened?

We computed the simple moving average for the close stock price. Truly, great riches are within your reach. It turns out that the simple moving average is just a signal processing technique—a convolution with weights $1 / N$, where N is the size of the moving average window. We learned that the ones function can create an array with ones and the convolve function calculates the convolution of a data set with specified weights (see sma.py).

```
import numpy as np
import sys
from matplotlib.pyplot import plot
from matplotlib.pyplot import show

N = int(sys.argv[1])

weights = np.ones(N) / N
print "Weights", weights

c = np.loadtxt('data.csv', delimiter=',', usecols=(6,), unpack=True)
sma = np.convolve(weights, c)[N-1:-N+1]
t = np.arange(N - 1, len(c))
```

```
plot(t, c[N-1:], lw=1.0)
plot(t, sma, lw=2.0)
show()
```

Exponential moving average

The exponential moving average is a popular alternative to the simple moving average. This method uses exponentially decreasing weights. The weights for points in the past decrease exponentially but never reach zero. We will learn about the exp and linspace functions while calculating the weights.

Time for action – calculating the exponential moving average

Given an array, the exp function calculates the exponential of each array element. For example, look at the following code:

```
x = np.arange(5)
print "Exp", np.exp(x)
```

It gives the following output:

```
Exp [  1.          2.71828183   7.3890561   20.08553692   54.59815003]
```

The linspace function takes, as parameters, a start and a stop and optionally an array size. It returns an array of evenly spaced numbers. The following is an example:

```
print "Linspace", np.linspace(-1, 0, 5)
```

This will give us the following output:

```
Linspace [-1.    -0.75 -0.5  -0.25  0.  ]
```

Let's calculate the exponential moving average for our data:

1. Now, back to the weights—calculate them with exp and linspace.

```
N = int(sys.argv[1])
weights = np.exp(np.linspace(-1., 0., N))
```

2. Normalize the weights. The ndarray object has a sum method that we will use.

```
weights /= weights.sum()
print "Weights", weights
```

For N = 5, we get the following weights:

```
Weights [ 0.11405072  0.14644403  0.18803785  0.24144538
 0.31002201]
```

3. After that, it's easy going—we just use the `convolve` function that we learned about in the simple moving average tutorial. We will also plot the results.

```
c = np.loadtxt('data.csv', delimiter=',', usecols=(6,),
unpack=True)
ema = np.convolve(weights, c)[N-1:-N+1]
t = np.arange(N - 1, len(c))
plot(t, c[N-1:], lw=1.0)
plot(t, ema, lw=2.0)
show()
```

That gives this nice chart where, again, the close price is the thin jagged line and the exponential moving average is the smooth thick line:

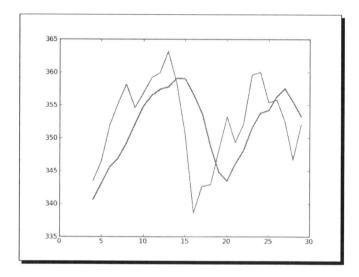

What just happened?

We calculated the exponential moving average of the close price. First, we computed exponentially decreasing weights with the `exp` and `linspace` functions. `linspace` gave us an array with evenly spaced elements, and then, we calculated the exponential for these numbers. We called the `ndarray sum` method in order to normalize the weights. After that, we applied the `convolve` trick that we learned in the simple moving average tutorial (see `ema.py`).

```
import numpy as np
import sys
from matplotlib.pyplot import plot
from matplotlib.pyplot import show

x = np.arange(5)
```

```
print "Exp", np.exp(x)
print "Linspace", np.linspace(-1, 0, 5)

N = int(sys.argv[1])


weights = np.exp(np.linspace(-1., 0., N))
weights /= weights.sum()
print "Weights", weights

c = np.loadtxt('data.csv', delimiter=',', usecols=(6,), unpack=True)
ema = np.convolve(weights, c)[N-1:-N+1]
t = np.arange(N - 1, len(c))
plot(t, c[N-1:], lw=1.0)
plot(t, ema, lw=2.0)
show()
```

Bollinger bands

Bollinger bands are yet another technical indicator. Yes, there are thousands of them. This one is named after its inventor and indicates a range for the price of a financial security. It consists of three parts, as follows:

- A simple moving average

- An upper band of two standard deviations above this moving average—the standard deviation is derived from the same data with which the moving average is calculated

- A lower band of two standard deviations below the moving average

Time for action – enveloping with Bollinger bands

We already know how to calculate the simple moving average. So, if you need to, please review the *Time for action – computing the simple moving average* section in this chapter. This example will introduce the NumPy `fill` function. The `fill` function sets the value of an array to a scalar value. The function should be faster than `array.flat = scalar` or you have to set the values of the array one by one in a loop. Perform the following steps to envelope with Bollinger bands:

1. Starting with an array called `sma` that contains the moving average values, we will loop through all the data sets corresponding to those values. After forming the data set, calculate the standard deviation. Note that it is necessary, at a certain point, to calculate the difference between each data point and the corresponding average value. If we did not have NumPy, we would loop through these points and subtract each of the values one by one from the corresponding average. However, the NumPy `fill` function allows us to construct an array having elements set to the same value. This enables us to save on one loop and subtract arrays in one go.

```
deviation = []
C = len(c)

for i in range(N - 1, C):
    if i + N < C:
        dev = c[i: i + N]
    else:
        dev = c[-N:]

    averages = np.zeros(N)
    averages.fill(sma[i - N - 1])
    dev = dev - averages
    dev = dev ** 2
    dev = np.sqrt(np.mean(dev))
    deviation.append(dev)

deviation = 2 * np.array(deviation)
upperBB = sma + deviation
lowerBB = sma - deviation
```

2. To plot the bands, we will use the following code (don't worry about it now; we will see how this works in *Chapter 9, Plotting with Matplotlib*):

```
t = numpy.arange(N - 1, C)
plot(t, c_slice, lw=1.0)
plot(t, sma, lw=2.0)
plot(t, upperBB, lw=3.0)
plot(t, lowerBB, lw=4.0)
show()
```

The following is a chart of the Bollinger bands for our data. The jagged thin line in the middle represents the close price and the slightly thicker, smoother line crossing it is the moving average:

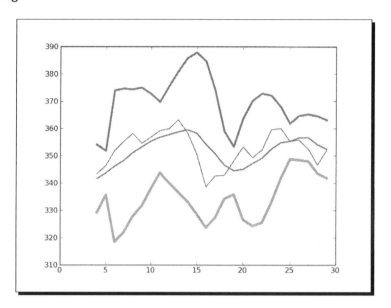

What just happened?

We worked out the Bollinger bands that envelope the close price of our data. More importantly, we got acquainted with the NumPy `fill` function. This function fills an array with a scalar value. This is the only parameter of the `fill` function (see `bollingerbands.py`).

```
import numpy as np
import sys
from matplotlib.pyplot import plot
from matplotlib.pyplot import show

N = int(sys.argv[1])

weights = np.ones(N) / N
print "Weights", weights

c = np.loadtxt('data.csv', delimiter=',', usecols=(6,), unpack=True)
sma = np.convolve(weights, c)[N-1:-N+1]
deviation = []
C = len(c)
```

```
for i in range(N - 1, C):
    if i + N < C:
      dev = c[i: i + N]
    else:
      dev = c[-N:]

    averages = np.zeros(N)
    averages.fill(sma[i - N - 1])
    dev = dev - averages
    dev = dev ** 2
    dev = np.sqrt(np.mean(dev))
    deviation.append(dev)

deviation = 2 * np.array(deviation)
print len(deviation), len(sma)
upperBB = sma + deviation
lowerBB = sma - deviation

c_slice = c[N-1:]
between_bands = np.where((c_slice < upperBB) & (c_slice > lowerBB))

print lowerBB[between_bands]
print c[between_bands]
print upperBB[between_bands]
between_bands = len(np.ravel(between_bands))
print "Ratio between bands", float(between_bands)/len(c_slice)

t = np.arange(N - 1, C)
plot(t, c_slice, lw=1.0)
plot(t, sma, lw=2.0)
plot(t, upperBB, lw=3.0)
plot(t, lowerBB, lw=4.0)
show()
```

Have a go hero – switching to exponential moving average

It is customary to choose the simple moving average to center the Bollinger band on. The second most popular choice is the exponential moving average, so try that as an exercise. You can find a suitable example in this chapter, if you need pointers.

Check that the `fill` function is faster or is as fast as `array.flat = scalar`, or set the value in a loop.

Linear model

Many phenomena in science have a related linear relationship model. The NumPy `linalg` package deals with linear algebra computations. We will begin with the assumption that a price value can be derived from *N* previous prices based on a linear relationship.

Time for action – predicting price with a linear model

Keeping an open mind, let's assume that we can express a stock price as a linear combination of previous values, that is, a sum of those values multiplied by certain coefficients we need to determine. In linear algebra terms, this boils down to finding a least squares solution. This recipe goes as follows.

1. First, form a vector `bbx` containing *N* price values.

   ```
   bbx = c [-N:]
   bbx = b[::-1]
   print "bbx", x
   ```

   The result is as follows:

   ```
   bbx [ 351.99  346.67  352.47  355.76  355.36]
   ```

2. Second, pre-initialize the matrix `A` to be *N x N* and containing zeroes.

   ```
   A = np.zeros((N, N), float)
   print "Zeros N by N", A
   Zeros N by N [[ 0.  0.  0.  0.  0.]
    [ 0.  0.  0.  0.  0.]
    [ 0.  0.  0.  0.  0.]
    [ 0.  0.  0.  0.  0.]
    [ 0.  0.  0.  0.  0.]]
   ```

3. Third, fill the matrix `A` with *N* preceding price values for each value in `bbx`.

   ```
   for i in range(N):
       A[i, ] = c[-N - 1 - i: - 1 - i]
   print "A", A
   ```

   Now, `A` looks like this:

   ```
   A [[ 360.     355.36  355.76  352.47  346.67]
    [ 359.56  360.     355.36  355.76  352.47]
    [ 352.12  359.56  360.     355.36  355.76]
    [ 349.31  352.12  359.56  360.     355.36]
    [ 353.21  349.31  352.12  359.56  360.   ]]
   ```

4. The objective is to determine the coefficients that satisfy our linear model, by solving the least squares problem. Employ the `lstsq` function of the NumPy `linalg` package to do that.

```
(x, residuals, rank, s) = np.linalg.lstsq(A, b)
```

```
print x, residuals, rank, s
```

The result is as follows:

```
[ 0.78111069 -1.44411737  1.63563225 -0.89905126  0.92009049]
[] 5 [  1.77736601e+03    1.49622969e+01    8.75528492e+00
5.15099261e+00    1.75199608e+00]
```

The tuple returned contains the coefficients xxb that we were after, an array comprising of residuals, the rank of matrix A, and the singular values of A.

5. Once we have the coefficients of our linear model, we can predict the next price value. Compute the dot product (with the NumPy `dot` function) of the coefficients and the last known *N* prices.

```
print numpy.dot(b, x)
```

The dot product is the linear combination of the coefficients xxb and the prices x. As a result, we get the following:

```
357.939161015
```

I looked it up; the actual close price of the next day was 353.56. So, our estimate with N = 5 was not that far off.

What just happened?

We predicted tomorrow's stock price today. If this works in practice, we could retire early! See, this book was a good investment after all! We designed a linear model for the predictions. The financial problem was reduced to a linear algebraic one. NumPy's `linalg` package has a practical `lstsq` function that helped us with the task at hand—estimating the coefficients of a linear model. After obtaining a solution, we plugged the numbers in the NumPy `dot` function that presented us an estimate through linear regression (see `linearmodel.py`).

```
import numpy as np
import sys

N = int(sys.argv[1])

c = np.loadtxt('data.csv', delimiter=',', usecols=(6,), unpack=True)
```

```
b = c[-N:]
b = b[::-1]
print "b", b

A = np.zeros((N, N), float)
print "Zeros N by N", A

for i in range(N):
   A[i, ] = c[-N - 1 - i: - 1 - i]

print "A", A


(x, residuals, rank, s) = np.linalg.lstsq(A, b)

print x, residuals, rank, s

print np.dot(b, x)
```

Trend lines

A **trend line** is a line among a number of so-called pivot points on a stock chart. As the name suggests, the line's trend portrays the trend of the price development. In the past, traders drew trend lines on paper; but, nowadays, we can let a computer draw it for us. In this tutorial, we shall resort to a very simple approach that is probably not very useful in real life, but it should clarify the principle well.

Time for action – drawing trend lines

Perform the following steps to draw trend lines:

> **1.** First, we need to determine the pivot points. We shall pretend they are equal to the arithmetic mean of the high, low, and close price.
>
> ```
> h, l, c = np.loadtxt('data.csv', delimiter=',', usecols=(4, 5,
> 6), unpack=True)
>
> pivots = (h + l + c) / 3
> print "Pivots", pivots
> ```
>
> From the pivots, we can deduce the so-called resistance and support levels. The support level is the lowest level at which the price rebounds. The resistance level is the highest level at which the price bounces back. These are not natural phenomena; mind you, they are merely estimates. Based on these estimates, it is possible to draw

support and resistance trend lines. We will define the daily spread to be the difference between the high and low price.

2. Define a function to fit line to data to a line where y = at + b. The function should return a and b. This is another opportunity to apply the lstsq function of the NumPy linalg package. Rewrite the line equation to y = Ax, where A = [t 1] and x = [a b]. Form A with the NumPy ones and vstack functions.

```
def fit_line(t, y):
    A = np.vstack([t, np.ones_like(t)])]).T
    return np.linalg.lstsq(A, y)[0]
```

3. Assuming that support levels are one daily spread below the pivots, and that resistance levels are one daily spread above the pivots, fit the support and resistance trend lines.

```
t = np.arange(len(c))
sa, sb = fit_line(t, pivots - (h - l))
ra, rb = fit_line(t, pivots + (h - l))
support = sa * t + sb
resistance = ra * t + rb
```

4. At this juncture, we have all the necessary information to draw the trend lines, however, it is wise to check how many points fall between the support and resistance levels. Obviously, if only a small percentage of the data is between the trend lines, this setup is of no use to us. Make up a condition for points between the bands and select the where function based on that condition.

```
condition = (c > support) & (c < resistance)
print "Condition", condition
between_bands = np.where(condition)
```

The following are the condition values:

```
Condition [False False   True   True   True   True   True False False
True False False
  False False False   True False False False   True   True   True   True
False False   True   True   True False   True]
```

Double-check the values:

```
print support[between_bands]
print c[between_bands]
print resistance[between_bands]
```

The array returned by the where function has rank 2, so call the ravel function before calling the len function.

```
between_bands = len(np.ravel(between_bands))
print "Number points between bands", between_bands
print "Ratio between bands", float(between_bands)/len(c)
```

You will get the following result:

```
Number points between bands 15
Ratio between bands 0.5
```

As an extra bonus, we gained a predictive model. Extrapolate the next day resistance and support levels.

```
print "Tomorrows support", sa * (t[-1] + 1) + sb
print "Tomorrows resistance", ra * (t[-1] + 1) + rb
```

This results in the following:

```
Tomorrows support 349.389157088
Tomorrows resistance 360.749340996
```

Another approach to figure out how many points are between the support and resistance estimates is to use [] and intersect1d. Define selection criteria in the [] operator and intersect the results with the intersect1d function.

```
a1 = c[c > support]
a2 = c[c < resistance]
print "Number of points between bands 2nd approach" ,len(np.
intersect1d(a1, a2))
```

Not surprisingly, we get the following:

```
Number of points between bands 2nd approach 15
```

5. Once more, we will plot the results, as follows:

```
plot(t, c)
plot(t, support)
plot(t, resistance)
show()
```

We will get the following plot in which we have the price data and the corresponding support and resistance lines:

What just happened?

We drew trend lines without having to mess around with rulers, pencils, and paper charts. We defined a function that can fit data to a line with the NumPy vstack, ones, and lstsq functions. We fit the data in order to define support and resistance trend lines. Then we figured out how many points are within the support and resistance range. We did this using two separate methods that produced the same result.

The first method used the where function with a Boolean condition. The second method made use of the [] operator and the intersect1d function. The intersect1d function returns an array of common elements from two arrays (see trendline.py).

```
import numpy as np
from matplotlib.pyplot import plot
from matplotlib.pyplot import show

def fit_line(t, y):
    A = np.vstack([t, np.ones_like(t)]).T

    return np.linalg.lstsq(A, y)[0]

h, l, c = np.loadtxt('data.csv', delimiter=',', usecols=(4, 5, 6),
unpack=True)
```

```
    pivots = (h + l + c) / 3
    print "Pivots", pivots

    t = np.arange(len(c))
    sa, sb = fit_line(t, pivots - (h - 1))
    ra, rb = fit_line(t, pivots + (h - 1))

    support = sa * t + sb
    resistance = ra * t + rb
    condition = (c > support) & (c < resistance)
    print "Condition", condition
    between_bands = np.where(condition)
    print support[between_bands]
    print c[between_bands]
    print resistance[between_bands]
    between_bands = len(np.ravel(between_bands))
    print "Number points between bands", between_bands
    print "Ratio between bands", float(between_bands)/len(c)

    print "Tomorrows support", sa * (t[-1] + 1) + sb
    print "Tomorrows resistance", ra * (t[-1] + 1) + rb

    a1 = c[c > support]
    a2 = c[c < resistance]
    print "Number of points between bands 2nd approach" ,len(np.
    intersect1d(a1, a2))

    plot(t, c)
    plot(t, support)
    plot(t, resistance)
    show()
```

Methods of ndarray

The NumPy ndarray class has a lot of methods that work on the array. Most of the time, these methods return an array. You may have noticed that many of the functions that are a part of the NumPy library have a counterpart with the same name and functionality in the ndarray object. This is mostly due to the historical development of NumPy.

The list of ndarray methods is pretty long, so we cannot cover them all. The var, sum, std, argmax, argmin, and mean functions that we saw earlier are also ndarray methods.

To clip and compress arrays, look at the following section.

Time for action – clipping and compressing arrays

Here are a few examples of `ndarray` methods. Perform the following steps to clip and compress arrays:

1. The `clip` method returns a clipped array, so that all values above a maximum value are set to the maximum and values below a minimum are set to the minimum value. Clip an array with values 0 to 4 to 1 and 2.

   ```
   a = np.arange(5)
   print "a =", a
   print "Clipped", a.clip(1, 2)
   ```

   This gives the following output:

   ```
   a = [0 1 2 3 4]
   Clipped [1 1 2 2 2]
   ```

2. The `ndarray compress` method returns an array based on a condition. For instance, look at the following code:

   ```
   a = np.arange(4)
   print a
   print "Compressed", a.compress(a > 2)
   ```

   This returns the following output:

   ```
   [0 1 2 3]
   Compressed [3]
   ```

What just happened?

We created an array with values 0 to 3 and selected the last element with the `compress` function based on the condition `a > 2`.

Factorial

Many programming books have an example of calculating the factorial. We should not break with this tradition.

Time for action – calculating the factorial

The `ndarray` class has the `prod` method, which computes the product of the elements in an array. Perform the following steps to calculate the factorial:

1. Calculate the factorial of eight. To do that, generate an array with values 1 to 8 and call the `prod` function on it.

```
b = np.arange(1, 9)
print "b =", b
print "Factorial", b.prod()
```

Check the result with your pocket calculator.

```
b = [1 2 3 4 5 6 7 8]
Factorial 40320
```

This is nice, but what if we want to know all the factorials from 1 to 8?

2. No problem! Call the `cumprod` method, which computes the cumulative product of an array.

```
print "Factorials", b.cumprod()
```

It's pocket calculator time again.

```
Factorials [    1    2    6   24  120  720 5040 40320]
```

What just happened?

We used the `prod` and `cumprod` functions to calculate factorials (see `ndarraymethods.py`).

```
import numpy as np

a = np.arange(5)
print "a =", a
print "Clipped", a.clip(1, 2)

a = np.arange(4)
print a
print "Compressed", a.compress(a > 2)

b = np.arange(1, 9)
print "b =", b
print "Factorial", b.prod()

print "Factorials", b.cumprod()
```

Summary

This chapter informed us about a great number of common NumPy functions. We read a file with `loadtxt` and wrote to a file with `savetxt`. We made an identity matrix with the `eye` function. We read a CSV file containing stock quotes with the `loadtxt` function. The NumPy `average` and `mean` functions allow one to calculate the weighted average and arithmetic mean of a data set.

A few common statistics functions were also mentioned – first, the `min` and `max` functions that we used to determine the range of the stock prices; second, the `median` function that gives the median of a data set; and finally, the `std` and `var` functions that return the standard deviation and variance of a set of numbers.

We calculated the simple stock returns with the `diff` function that returns back the differences between sequential elements. The `log` function computes the natural logarithms of array elements.

By default, `loadtxt` tries to convert all data into floats. The `loadtxt` function has a special parameter for this purpose. The parameter is called `converters` and is a dictionary that links columns with the so-called converter functions.

We defined a function and passed it as an argument to the `apply_along_axis` function. We implemented an algorithm with the requirement to find the maximum value across arrays.

We learned that the `ones` function can create an array with ones and the `convolve` function calculates the convolution of a data set with the specified weights.

We computed exponentially decreasing weights with the `exp` and `linspace` functions. `linspace` gave us an array with evenly spaced elements, and then we calculated the exponential for these numbers. We called the `ndarray sum` method in order to normalize the weights.

We got acquainted with the NumPy `fill` function. This function fills an array with a scalar value, the only parameter of the `fill` function.

After this tour through the common NumPy functions, we will continue covering convenience NumPy functions such as `polyfit`, `sign`, and `piecewise` in the next chapter.

4
Convenience Functions for Your Convenience

As we have noticed, NumPy has a great number of functions. Many of these functions are there just for your convenience. Knowing these functions will greatly increase your productivity. This includes functions that select certain parts of your arrays (for instance, based on a Boolean condition) or manipulate polynomials. An example of computing correlation of stock returns is provided to give you a taste of data analysis in NumPy.

In this chapter, we shall cover the following topics:

- ◆ Data selection and extraction
- ◆ Simple data analysis
- ◆ Examples of correlation of returns
- ◆ Polynomials
- ◆ Linear algebra functions

In the previous chapter, we had one single data file to play around with. Things have significantly improved in this chapter—we now have two data files. Let's go ahead and explore the data with NumPy.

Correlation

Have you noticed that the stock price of some companies is closely followed by another one, usually a rival in the same sector? The theoretical explanation is that, because these two companies are in the same type of business, they share the same challenges, require the same materials and resources, and compete for the same type of customers.

You could think of many possible pairs, but you would want to check whether a real relationship exists. One way is to have a look at the correlation of the stock returns of both stocks. A high correlation implies a relationship of some sort. It is not proof though, especially if you don't use sufficient data.

Time for action – trading correlated pairs

For this tutorial, we will use two sample data sets, containing the bare minimum of end-of-day price data. The first company is BHP Billiton (BHP), which is active in the mining of petroleum, metals, and diamonds. The second is Vale (VALE), which is also a metals and mining company. So there is some overlap, albeit not one hundred percent. For trading correlated pairs, follow these steps:

1. First, load the data, specifically the close price of the two securities, from the CSV files in the example code directory of this chapter and calculate the returns. If you don't remember how to do it, there are plenty of examples in the previous chapter.

2. Covariance tells us how two variables vary together; it is nothing more than unnormalized correlation. Compute the covariance matrix from the returns with the `cov` function (it's not strictly necessary to do this, but it will allow us to demonstrate a few matrix operations):

```
covariance = np.cov(bhp_returns, vale_returns)
print "Covariance", covariance
```

The covariance matrix is as follows:

```
Covariance [[ 0.00028179  0.00019766]
            [ 0.00019766  0.00030123]]
```

3. View the values on the diagonal with the `diagonal` function:

```
print "Covariance diagonal", covariance.diagonal()
```

The diagonal values of the covariance matrix are as follows:

```
Covariance diagonal [ 0.00028179  0.00030123]
```

Notice that the values on the diagonal are not equal to each other, this is different from the correlation matrix.

4. Compute the trace, the sum of the diagonal values, with the `trace` function:

```
print "Covariance trace", covariance.trace()
```

The trace values of the covariance matrix are as follows:

```
Covariance trace  0.00058302354992
```

5. The correlation of two vectors is defined as the covariance, divided by the product of the respective standard deviations of the vectors. The equation for vectors a and b is:

$$corr(a,b) = \frac{cov(a,b)}{\sigma_b\ \sigma_b}$$

Try it out:

```
print covariance/ (bhp_returns.std() * vale_returns.std())
```

The correlation matrix is as follows:

```
[[ 1.00173366  0.70264666]
 [ 0.70264666  1.0708476 ]]
```

6. We will measure the correlation of our pair with the correlation coefficient. The correlation coefficient takes values between -1 to 1. The correlation of a set of values with itself is 1 by definition. This would be the ideal value; however, we will be also happy with a slightly lower value. Calculate the correlation coefficient (or, more accurately, the correlation matrix) with the `corrcoef` function:

```
print "Correlation coefficient", np.corrcoef(bhp_returns,
vale_returns)
```

The coefficients are as follows:

```
[[ 1.          0.67841747]
 [ 0.67841747  1.          ]]
```

The values on the diagonal are just the correlations of the BHP and VALE with themselves and are, therefore, equal to 1. In all probability, no real calculation takes place. The other two values are equal to each other since correlation is symmetrical, meaning that the correlation of BHP with VALE is equal to the correlation of VALE with BHP. It seems that the correlation is not that strong.

7. Another important point is whether the two stocks under consideration are in sync or not. Two stocks are considered out of sync if their difference is two standard deviations from the mean of the differences.

If they are out of sync, we could initiate a trade, hoping that they eventually will get back in sync again. Compute the difference between the close prices of the two securities to check the synchronization:

```
difference = bhp - vale
```

Check whether the last difference in price is out of sync; see the following code:

```
avg = np.mean(difference)
dev = np.std(difference)
print "Out of sync", np.abs(difference[-1] - avg) > 2 * dev
```

Unfortunately, we cannot trade yet:

```
Out of sync False
```

8. Plotting requires `Matplotlib`; this will be discussed in *Chapter 9, Plotting with Matplotlib*. Plotting can be done as follows:

```
t = np.arange(len(bhp_returns))
plot(t, bhp_returns, lw=1)
plot(t, vale_returns, lw=2)
show()
```

The resulting plot:

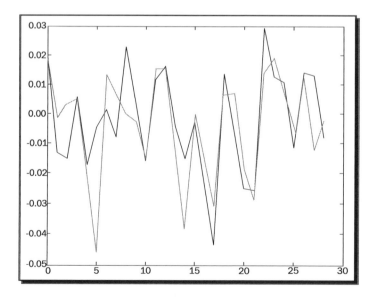

What just happened?

We analyzed the relation of the closing stock prices of BHP and VALE. To be precise, we calculated the correlation of their stock returns. This was achieved with the `corrcoef` function. Further, we saw how the covariance matrix can be computed, from which the correlation can be derived. As a bonus, a demonstration was given of the `diagonal` and `trace` functions that can give us the diagonal values and the trace of a matrix, respectively (see `correlation.py`):

```python
import numpy as np
from matplotlib.pyplot import plot
from matplotlib.pyplot import show

bhp = np.loadtxt('BHP.csv', delimiter=',', usecols=(6,), unpack=True)

bhp_returns = np.diff(bhp) / bhp[ : -1]

vale = np.loadtxt('VALE.csv', delimiter=',', usecols=(6,),
unpack=True)

vale_returns = np.diff(vale) / vale[ : -1]

covariance = np.cov(bhp_returns, vale_returns)
print "Covariance", covariance

print "Covariance diagonal", covariance.diagonal()
print "Covariance trace", covariance.trace()

print covariance/ (bhp_returns.std() * vale_returns.std())

print "Correlation coefficient", np.corrcoef(bhp_returns, vale_
returns)

difference = bhp - vale
avg = np.mean(difference)
dev = np.std(difference)

print "Out of sync", np.abs(difference[-1] - avg) > 2 * dev

t = np.arange(len(bhp_returns))
plot(t, bhp_returns, lw=1)
plot(t, vale_returns, lw=2)
show()
```

Pop quiz – calculating covariance

Q1. Which function returns the covariance of two arrays?

1. covariance
2. covar
3. cov
4. cvar

Polynomials

Do you like calculus? Me, I love it! One of the ideas in calculus is Taylor expansion, that is, representing a differentiable function as an infinite series. In practice, this means that any differentiable, and therefore, continuous function can be estimated by a polynomial of a high degree. The terms of the higher degree would then be assumed to be negligibly small.

Time for action – fitting to polynomials

The NumPy `polyfit` function can fit a set of data points to a polynomial even if the underlying function is not continuous:

1. Continuing with the price data of BHP and VALE, let's look at the difference of their close prices and fit it to a polynomial of the third power:

```
bhp=np.loadtxt('BHP.csv', delimiter=',', usecols=(6,),
    unpack=True)
vale=np.loadtxt('VALE.csv', delimiter=',', usecols=(6,),
    unpack=True)
t = np.arange(len(bhp))
poly = np.polyfit(t, bhp - vale, int(sys.argv[1]))
print "Polynomial fit", poly
```

The polynomial fit (in this example, a cubic polynomial was chosen):

```
Polynomial fit [  1.11655581e-03   -5.28581762e-02
5.80684638e-01    5.79791202e+01]
```

2. The numbers you see are the coefficients of the polynomial. Extrapolate to the next value with the `polyval` function and the polynomial object we got from the fit:

```
print "Next value", np.polyval(poly, t[-1] + 1)
```

The next value we predict will be:

```
Next value 57.9743076081
```

3. Ideally, the difference between the close prices of BHP and VALE should be as small as possible. In an extreme case, it might be zero at some point. Find out when our polynomial fit reaches zero with the `roots` function:

```
print "Roots", np.roots(poly)
```

The roots of the polynomial are as follows:

```
Roots [ 35.48624287+30.62717062j   35.48624287-30.62717062j
 -23.63210575 +0.j            ]
```

4. Another thing we learned in calculus class was to find extrema—these could be potential maxima or minima. Remember, from calculus, that these are the points where the derivative of our function is zero. Differentiate the polynomial fit with the `polyder` function:

```
der = np.polyder(poly)
print "Derivative", der
```

The coefficients of the derivative polynomial are as follows:

```
Derivative [ 0.00334967 -0.10571635  0.58068464]
```

The numbers you see are the coefficients of the derivative polynomial.

5. Get the roots of the derivative and find the extrema:

```
print "Extremas", np.roots(der)
```

The extrema that we get are:

```
Extremas [ 24.47820054   7.08205278]
```

Let's double check; compute the values of the fit with `polyval`:

```
vals = np.polyval(poly, t)
```

6. Now, find the maximum and minimum values with `argmax` and `argmin`:

```
vals = np.polyval(poly, t)
print np.argmax(vals)
print np.argmin(vals)
```

This gives us the following expected results. Ok, not quite the same results, but, if we backtrack to step 1, we can see that t was defined with the `arange` function:

```
7
24
```

7. Plot the data and the fit it as follows:

```
plot(t, bhp - vale)
plot(t, vals)
show()
```

It results in this plot:

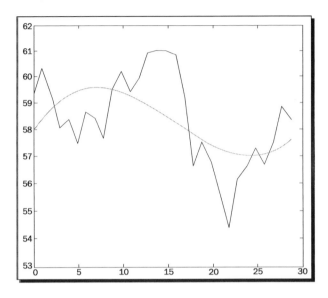

Obviously, the smooth line is the fit and the jagged line is the underlying data. It's not that good a fit, so you might want to try a higher order polynomial.

What just happened?

We fit data to a polynomial with the `polyfit` function. We learned about the `polyval` function that computes the values of a polynomial, the `roots` function that returns the roots of the polynomial, and the `polyder` function that gives back the derivative of a polynomial (see `polynomials.py`):

```
import numpy as np
import sys
from matplotlib.pyplot import plot
from matplotlib.pyplot import show

bhp=np.loadtxt('BHP.csv', delimiter=',', usecols=(6,),
unpack=True)

vale=np.loadtxt('VALE.csv', delimiter=',', usecols=(6,),
unpack=True)
```

```
t = np.arange(len(bhp))
poly = np.polyfit(t, bhp - vale, int(sys.argv[1]))
print "Polynomial fit", poly

print "Next value", np.polyval(poly, t[-1] + 1)

print "Roots", np.roots(poly)

der = np.polyder(poly)
print "Derivative", der

print "Extremas", np.roots(der)
vals = np.polyval(poly, t)
print np.argmax(vals)
print np.argmin(vals)

plot(t, bhp - vale)
plot(t, vals)
show()
```

Have a go hero – improving the fit

There are a number of things you could do to improve the fit. Try a different power as, in this tutorial, a cubic polynomial was chosen. Consider smoothing the data before fitting it. One way you could smooth is with a moving average. Examples of simple and exponential moving average calculations can be found in the previous chapter.

On-balance volume

Volume is a very important variable in investing; it indicates how big a price move is. The on-balance volume indicator is one of the simplest stock price indicators. It is based on the close price of the current and previous days and the volume of the current day. For each day, if the close price today is higher than the close price of yesterday then the value of the on-balance volume is equal to the volume of today. On the other hand, if today's close price is lower than yesterday's close price then the value of the on-balance volume indicator is the difference between the on-balance volume and the volume of today. If the close price did not change then the value of the on-balance volume is zero.

Time for action – balancing volume

In other words we need to multiply the sign of the close price with the volume. In this tutorial, we will go over two approaches to this problem, one using the NumPy `sign` function, and the other using the NumPy `piecewise` function.

1. Load the BHP data into a close and volume array:

```
c, v=np.loadtxt('BHP.csv', delimiter=',', usecols=(6, 7),
    unpack=True)
```

Compute the absolute value changes. Calculate the change of the close price with the `diff` function. The `diff` function computes the difference between two sequential array elements and returns an array containing these differences:

```
change = np.diff(c)
print "Change", change
```

The changes of the close price are shown as follows:

```
Change [ 1.92 -1.08 -1.26  0.63 -1.54 -0.28  0.25 -0.6    2.15
0.69 -1.33   1.16
   1.59 -0.26 -1.29 -0.13 -2.12 -3.91  1.28 -0.57 -2.07 -2.07
2.5    1.18
-0.88   1.31   1.24 -0.59]
```

2. The NumPy `sign` function returns the signs for each element in an array. `-1` is returned for a negative number, `1` for a positive number, and `0`, otherwise. Apply the `sign` function to the `change` array:

```
signs = np.sign(change)
print "Signs", signs
```

The signs of the change array are as follows:

```
Signs [ 1. -1. -1.  1. -1. -1.  1. -1.  1.  1. -1.  1.  1. -1. -1.
-1. -1. -1.
-1. -1. -1.  1.  1.  1. -1.  1.  1. -1.]
```

Alternatively, we can calculate the signs with the `piecewise` function. The `piecewise` function, as its name suggests, evaluates a function piece-by-piece. Call the function with the appropriate return values and conditions:

```
pieces = np.piecewise(change, [change < 0, change > 0], [-1,
    1])
print "Pieces", pieces
```

The signs are shown again, as follows:

```
Pieces [ 1. -1. -1.  1. -1. -1.  1. -1.  1.  1. -1.  1.  1. -1.
-1. -1. -1. -1.
-1. -1. -1.  1.  1.  1. -1.  1.  1. -1.]
```

Check that the outcome is the same:

```
print "Arrays equal?", np.array_equal(signs, pieces)
```

And the outcome is as follows:

```
Arrays equal? True
```

3. The on-balance volume depends on the change of the previous close, so we cannot calculate it for the first day in our sample:

```
print "On balance volume", v[1:] * signs
```

The on-balance volume is as follows:

```
[ 2620800. -2461300. -3270900.  2650200. -4667300. -5359800.
7768400.
 -4799100.  3448300.  4719800. -3898900.  3727700.  3379400.
-2463900.
 -3590900. -3805000. -3271700. -5507800.  2996800. -3434800.
-5008300.
 -7809799.  3947100.  3809700.  3098200. -3500200.  4285600.
3918800.
 -3632200.]
```

What just happened?

We computed the on-balance volume that depends on the change of the closing price. Using the NumPy `sign` and `piecewise` functions, we went over two different methods to determine the sign of the change (see `obv.py`):

```
import numpy as np

c, v=np.loadtxt('BHP.csv', delimiter=',', usecols=(6, 7), unpack=True)

change = np.diff(c)
print "Change", change

signs = np.sign(change)
print "Signs", signs
```

```
pieces = np.piecewise(change, [change < 0, change > 0], [-1, 1])
print "Pieces", pieces

print "Arrays equal?", np.array_equal(signs, pieces)

print "On balance volume", v[1:] * signs
```

Simulation

Often, you would want to try something out. Play around, experiment, but preferably without blowing things up or getting dirty. NumPy is perfect for experimentation. We will use NumPy to simulate a trading day, without actually losing money. Many people like to buy on the dip or, in other words, wait for the price of stocks to drop before buying. A variant of that is to wait for the price to drop a small percentage, say, 0.1 percent below the opening price of the day.

Time for action – avoiding loops with vectorize

The vectorize function is a yet another trick to reduce the number of loops in your programs. We will let it calculate the profit of a single trading day:

1. First, load the data:

   ```
   o, h, l, c = np.loadtxt('BHP.csv', delimiter=',', usecols=(3,
   4, 5, 6), unpack=True)
   ```

2. The vectorize function is the NumPy equivalent of the Python map function. Call the vectorize function, giving it as an argument the calc_profit function that we still have to write:

   ```
   func = np.vectorize(calc_profit)
   ```

3. We can now apply func as if it is a function. Apply the func result that we got, to the price arrays:

   ```
   profits = func(o, h, l, c)
   ```

4. The calc_profit function is pretty simple. First, we try to buy slightly below the open price. If this is outside of the daily range, then, obviously our attempt failed and no profit was made, or we incurred a loss, therefore, we will return 0. Otherwise, we sell at the close price and the profit is just the difference between the buy price and the close price. Actually, it is more interesting to have a look at the relative profit:

   ```
   def calc_profit((open, high, low, close):
       #buy just below the open
       buy = open * float(sys.argv[1])
       # daily range
   ```

```
    if low <  buy < high:
        return (close - buy)/buy
    else:
        return 0
print "Profits", profits
```

5. There are two days with zero profits: there was either no net gain, or a loss. Select the days with trades and calculate averages:

```
real_trades = profits[profits != 0]
print "Number of trades", len(real_trades), round(100.0 *
len(real_trades)/len(c), 2), "%"
print "Average profit/loss %", round(np.mean(real_trades) *
100, 2)
```

The trades summary are shown as follows:

```
Number of trades 28 93.33 %
Average profit/loss % 0.02
```

6. As optimists, we are interested in winning trades with a gain greater than zero. Select the days with winning trades and calculate averages:

```
winning_trades = profits[profits > 0]
print "Number of winning trades", len(winning_trades),
round(100.0
  * len(winning_trades)/len(c), 2), "%"
print "Average profit %", round(np.mean(winning_trades) * 100,
  2)
```

The winning trades are:

```
Number of winning trades 16 53.33 %
Average profit % 0.72
```

7. As pessimists, we are interested in losing trades with profit less than zero. Select the days with losing trades and calculate averages:

```
losing_trades = profits[profits < 0]
print "Number of losing trades", len(losing_trades),
round(100.0 *
  len(losing_trades)/len(c), 2), "%"
print "Average loss %", round(np.mean(losing_trades) * 100, 2)
```

The losing trades are:

```
Number of losing trades 12 40.0 %
Average loss % -0.92
```

What just happened?

We vectorized a function, which is just another way to avoid using loops. We simulated a trading day with a function, which returned the relative profit of each day's trade. We printed a summary of the losing and winning trades (see `simulation.py`):

```
import numpy as np
import sys

o, h, l, c = np.loadtxt('BHP.csv', delimiter=',', usecols=(3, 4, 5,
6), unpack=True)

def calc_profit(open, high, low, close):
    #buy just below the open
    buy = open * float(sys.argv[1])

    # daily range
    if low <  buy < high:
        return (close - buy)/buy
    else:
        return 0

func = np.vectorize(calc_profit)
profits = func(o, h, l, c)
print "Profits", profits

real_trades = profits[profits != 0]
print "Number of trades", len(real_trades), round(100.0 * len(real_
trades)/len(c), 2), "%"
print "Average profit/loss %", round(np.mean(real_trades) * 100, 2)

winning_trades = profits[profits > 0]
print "Number of winning trades", len(winning_trades), round(100.0 *
len(winning_trades)/len(c), 2), "%"
print "Average profit %", round(np.mean(winning_trades) * 100, 2)

losing_trades = profits[profits < 0]
print "Number of losing trades", len(losing_trades), round(100.0 *
len(losing_trades)/len(c), 2), "%"
print "Average loss %", round(np.mean(losing_trades) * 100, 2)
```

Have a go hero – analyzing consecutive wins and losses

Although the average profit is positive, it is also important to know whether we had to endure a long streak of consecutive losses. If this is the case, we might be left with little or no capital, and then the average profit would not matter that much.

Find out if there was such a losing streak. If you want, you can also find out if there was a prolonged winning streak.

Smoothing

Noisy data is difficult to deal with, so we often need to do some smoothing. Besides calculating moving averages, we can use one of the NumPy functions to smooth data.

The `hanning` function is a windowing function formed by a weighted cosine. There are other window functions that will be covered in greater detail in later chapters.

Time for action – smoothing with the hanning function

We will use the `hanning` function to smooth arrays of stock returns, as shown in the following steps:

1. Call the `hanning` function to compute weights, for a certain N length window (in this example, N is 8):

```
N = int(sys.argv[1])
weights = np.hanning(N)
print "Weights", weights
```

The weights are as follows:

```
Weights [ 0.          0.1882551   0.61126047  0.95048443
0.95048443  0.61126047
  0.1882551   0.          ]
```

2. Calculate the stock returns for the BHP and VALE quotes using `convolve` with normalized `weights`:

```
bhp = np.loadtxt('BHP.csv', delimiter=',', usecols=(6,),
  unpack=True)
bhp_returns = np.diff(bhp) / bhp[ : -1]
smooth_bhp = np.convolve(weights/weights.sum(), bhp_returns)
  [N-1:-N+1]
vale = np.loadtxt('VALE.csv', delimiter=',', usecols=(6,),
  unpack=True)
vale_returns = np.diff(vale) / vale[ : -1]
smooth_vale = np.convolve(weights/weights.sum(), vale_returns)
  [N-1:-N+1]
```

3. Plotting with `Matplotlib`:

```
t = np.arange(N - 1, len(bhp_returns))
plot(t, bhp_returns[N-1:], lw=1.0)
plot(t, smooth_bhp, lw=2.0)
plot(t, vale_returns[N-1:], lw=1.0)
plot(t, smooth_vale, lw=2.0)
show()
```

The chart would appear as follows:

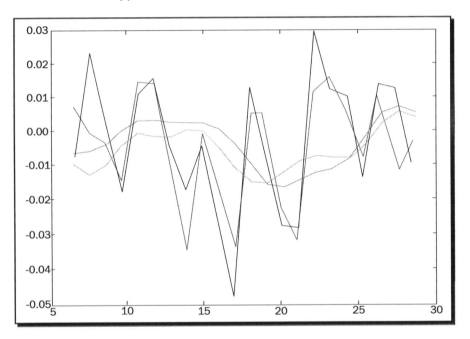

The thin lines on the chart are the stock returns and the thick lines are the result of smoothing. As you can see, the lines cross a few times. These points might be important, because the trend might have changed there. Or, at least, the relation of BHP to VALE might have changed. These turning inflection points probably occur often, so we might want to project into the future.

4. Fit the result of the smoothing step to polynomials:

```
K = int(sys.argv[1])
t = np.arange(N - 1, len(bhp_returns))
poly_bhp = np.polyfit(t, smooth_bhp, K)
poly_vale = np.polyfit(t, smooth_vale, K)
```

5. Now, we need to compute for a situation where the polynomials we found in the previous step are equal to each other. This boils down to subtracting the polynomials and finding the roots of the resulting polynomial. Subtract the polynomials using `polysub`:

```
poly_sub = np.polysub(poly_bhp, poly_vale)
xpoints = np.roots(poly_sub)
print "Intersection points", xpoints
```

The points are shown as follows:

```
Intersection points [ 27.73321597+0.j        27.51284094+0.j
24.32064343+0.j
  18.86423973+0.j         12.43797190+1.73218179j  12.43797190-
1.73218179j
   6.34613053+0.62519463j   6.34613053-0.62519463j]
```

6. The numbers we get are complex; that is not good for us, unless there is such a thing as imaginary time. Check which numbers are real with the `isreal` function:

```
reals = np.isreal(xpoints)
print "Real number?", reals
```

The result is as follows:

```
Real number? [ True   True   True   True False False False False]
```

Some of the numbers are real, so select them with the select function. The `select` function forms an array by taking elements from a list of choices, based on a list of conditions:

```
xpoints = np.select([reals], [xpoints])
xpoints = xpoints.real
print "Real intersection points", xpoints
```

The real intersection points are as follows:

```
Real intersection points [ 27.73321597   27.51284094
24.32064343   18.86423973    0.        0.    0.    0.]
```

7. We managed to pick up some zeroes. The `trim_zeros` function strips the leading and trailing zeros from a one-dimensional array. Get rid of the zeroes with `trim_zeros`:

```
print "Sans 0s", np.trim_zeros(xpoints)
```

The zeroes are gone, and the output is shown as follows:

```
Sans 0s [ 27.73321597   27.51284094   24.32064343   18.86423973]
```

What just happened?

We applied the `hanning` function to smooth arrays containing stock returns. We subtracted two polynomials with the `polysub` function. We checked for real numbers with the `isreal` function and selected the real numbers with the `select` function. Finally, we stripped zeroes from an array with the `strip_zeroes` function (see `smoothing.py`):

```python
import numpy as np
import sys
from matplotlib.pyplot import plot
from matplotlib.pyplot import show

N = int(sys.argv[1])

weights = np.hanning(N)
print "Weights", weights

bhp = np.loadtxt('BHP.csv', delimiter=',', usecols=(6,), unpack=True)
bhp_returns = np.diff(bhp) / bhp[ : -1]
smooth_bhp = np.convolve(weights/weights.sum(), bhp_returns)[N-1:
-N+1]

vale = np.loadtxt('VALE.csv', delimiter=',', usecols=(6,), un
pack=True)
vale_returns = np.diff(vale) / vale[ : -1]
smooth_vale = np.convolve(weights/weights.sum(), vale_returns)[N-1:
-N+1]

K = int(sys.argv[1])
t = np.arange(N - 1, len(bhp_returns))
poly_bhp = np.polyfit(t, smooth_bhp, K)
poly_vale = np.polyfit(t, smooth_vale, K)

poly_sub = np.polysub(poly_bhp, poly_vale)
xpoints = np.roots(poly_sub)
print "Intersection points", xpoints

reals = np.isreal(xpoints)
print "Real number?", reals

xpoints = np.select([reals], [xpoints])
xpoints = xpoints.real
print "Real intersection points", xpoints
```

```
print "Sans 0s", np.trim_zeros(xpoints)

plot(t, bhp_returns[N-1:], lw=1.0)
plot(t, smooth_bhp, lw=2.0)

plot(t, vale_returns[N-1:], lw=1.0)
plot(t, smooth_vale, lw=2.0)
show()
```

Have a go hero – smoothing variations

Experiment with the other smoothing functions—hamming, blackman, bartlett, and kaiser. They work more or less in the same way as hanning.

Summary

We calculated the correlation of the stock returns of two stocks with the corrcoef function. As a bonus, a demonstration of the diagonal and trace functions was given, which can give us the diagonal and trace of a matrix.

We fit data to a polynomial with the polyfit function. We learned about the polyval function that computes the values of a polynomial, the roots function that returns the roots of the polynomial, and the polyder function that gives back the derivative of a polynomial.

Hopefully, we increased our productivity so that we can continue in the next chapter with matrices and universal functions (ufuncs).

5

Working with Matrices and ufuncs

*This chapter covers matrices and **universal functions** (ufuncs). Matrices are well known in mathematics and have their representation in NumPy as well. Universal functions work on arrays, element-by-element, or on scalars. ufuncs expect a set of scalars as input and produce a set of scalars as output. Universal functions can typically be mapped to mathematical counterparts, such as add, subtract, divide, multiply, and likewise. We will also be introduced to trigonometric, bitwise, and comparison universal functions.*

In this chapter, we shall cover the following topics:

- ◆ Matrix creation
- ◆ Matrix operations
- ◆ Basic ufuncs
- ◆ Trigonometric functions
- ◆ Bitwise functions
- ◆ Comparison functions

Matrices

Matrices in NumPy are subclasses of `ndarray`. Matrices can be created using a special string format. They are, just like in mathematics, two-dimensional. Matrix multiplication is, as you would expect, different from the normal NumPy multiplication. The same is true for the power operator. We can create matrices with the `mat`, `matrix`, and `bmat` functions.

Time for action – creating matrices

Matrices can be created with the `mat` function. This function does not make a copy if the input is already a `matrix` or an `ndarray`. Calling this function is equivalent to calling `matrix(data, copy=False)`. We will also demonstrate transposing and inverting matrices.

1. Rows are delimited by a semicolon, values by a space. Call the `mat` function with the following string to create a matrix:

```
A = np.mat('1 2 3; 4 5 6; 7 8 9')
print "Creation from string", A
```

The matrix output should be the following matrix:

```
Creation from string [[1 2 3]
 [4 5 6]
 [7 8 9]]
```

2. Transpose the matrix with the `T` attribute, as follows:

```
print "transpose A", A.T
```

The following is the transposed matrix:

```
transpose A [[1 4 7]
 [2 5 8]
 [3 6 9]]
```

3. The matrix can be inverted with the `I` attribute, as follows:

```
print "Inverse A", A.I
```

The inverse matrix is printed as follows (be warned that this is a $O(n3)$ operation):

```
Inverse A [[ -4.50359963e+15   9.00719925e+15  -4.50359963e+15]
 [  9.00719925e+15  -1.80143985e+16   9.00719925e+15]
 [ -4.50359963e+15   9.00719925e+15  -4.50359963e+15]]
```

4. Instead of using a string to create a matrix, let's do it with an array:

```
print "Creation from array", np.mat(np.arange(9).reshape(3, 3))
```

The newly-created array is printed as follows:

```
Creation from array [[0 1 2]
 [3 4 5]
 [6 7 8]]
```

What just happened?

We created matrices with the `mat` function. We transposed the matrices with the `T` attribute and inverted them with the `I` attribute (see `matrixcreation.py`):

```
import numpy as np

A = np.mat('1 2 3; 4 5 6; 7 8 9')
print "Creation from string", A
print "transpose A", A.T
print "Inverse A", A.I
print "Check Inverse", A * A.I

print "Creation from array", np.mat(np.arange(9).reshape(3, 3))
```

Creating a matrix from other matrices

Sometimes we want to create a matrix from other smaller matrices. We can do this with the `bmat` function. The `b` here stands for block matrix.

Time for action – creating a matrix from other matrices

We will create a matrix from two smaller matrices, as follows:

1. First create a two-by-two identity matrix:

    ```
    A = np.eye(2)
    print "A", A
    ```

    The identity matrix looks like this:

    ```
    A [[ 1.  0.]
     [ 0.  1.]]
    ```

    Create another matrix like `A` and multiply by `2`:

    ```
    B = 2 * A
    print "B", B
    ```

    The second matrix is as follows:

    ```
    B [[ 2.  0.]
     [ 0.  2.]]
    ```

2. Create the compound matrix from a string. The string uses the same format as the `mat` function; only, you can use matrices instead of numbers.

```
print "Compound matrix\n", np.bmat("A B; A B")
```

The compound matrix is shown as follows:

```
Compound matrix
[[ 1.  0.  2.  0.]
 [ 0.  1.  0.  2.]
 [ 1.  0.  2.  0.]
 [ 0.  1.  0.  2.]]
```

What just happened?

We created a block matrix from two smaller matrices, with the `bmat` function. We gave the function a string containing the names of matrices instead of numbers (see `bmatcreation.py`):

```
import numpy as np

A = np.eye(2)
print "A", A
B = 2 * A
print "B", B
print "Compound matrix\n", np.bmat("A B; A B")
```

Pop quiz – defining a matrix with a string

Q1. What is the row delimiter in a string accepted by the `mat` and `bmat` functions?

1. Semicolon
2. Colon
3. Comma
4. Space

Universal functions

Ufuncs expect a set of scalars as input and produce a set of scalars as output. Universal functions can typically be mapped to mathematical counterparts, such as, add, subtract, divide, multiply, and likewise.

Time for action – creating universal function

We can create a universal function from a Python function with the NumPy `frompyfunc` function, as follows:

1. Define a Python function that answers the ultimate question to the universe, existence, and the rest (it's from *The Hitchhiker's Guide to the Galaxy*; if you haven't read it, you can safely ignore this).

```
def ultimate_answer(a):
```

So far, nothing special; we gave the function the name `ultimate_answer` and defined one parameter, `a`.

2. Create a result consisting of all zeros, that has the same shape as `a`, with the `zeros_like` function:

```
result = np.zeros_like(a)
```

3. Now set the elements of the initialized array to the answer `42` and return the result. The complete function should appear as shown, in the following code snippet. The `flat` attribute gives us access to a flat iterator that allows us to set the value of the array:

```
def ultimate_answer(a):
    result = np.zeros_like(a)
    result.flat = 42
    return result
```

4. Create a universal function with `frompyfunc`; specify `1` as as number of input parameter followed by `1` as the number of output parameters:

```
ufunc = np.frompyfunc(ultimate_answer, 1, 1)
print "The answer", ufunc(np.arange(4))
```

The result for a one-dimensional array is shown as follows:

The answer [42 42 42 42]

We can do the same for a two-dimensional array by using the following code:

```
print "The answer", ufunc(np.arange(4).reshape(2, 2))
```

The output for a two dimensional array is shown as follows

The answer [[42 42]
           [[42 42]

           [42 42]]

What just happened?

We defined a Python function. In this function, we initialized to zero the elements of an array, based on the shape of an input argument, with the `zeros_like` function. Then, with the `flat` attribute of `ndarray`, we set the array elements to the ultimate answer, 42 (see `answer42.py`):

```
import numpy as np

def ultimate_answer(a):
    result = np.zeros_like(a)
    result.flat = 42

    return result

ufunc = np.frompyfunc(ultimate_answer, 1, 1)
print "The answer", ufunc(np.arange(4))

print "The answer", ufunc(np.arange(4).reshape(2, 2))
```

Universal function methods

How can functions have methods? As we said earlier, universal functions are not functions but objects representing functions. Universal functions have four methods. They only make sense for functions such as `add`. That is, they have two input parameters and return one output parameter. If the signature of an ufunc does not match this condition, this will result in a `ValueError`, so call this method only for binary universal functions. The four methods are listed as follows:

- `reduce`
- `accumulate`
- `reduceat`
- `outer`

Time for action – applying the ufunc methods on add

Let's call the four methods on `add` function.

1. The input array is reduced by applying the universal function recursively along a specified axis on consecutive elements. For the `add` function, the result of reducing is similar to calculating the sum of an array. Call the `reduce` method:

```
a = np.arange(9)
print "Reduce", np.add.reduce(a)
```

The reduced array should be as follows:

```
Reduce 36
```

2. The `accumulate` method also recursively goes through the input array. But, contrary to the `reduce` method, it stores the intermediate results in an array and returns that. The result, in the case of the `add` function, is equivalent to calling the `cumsum` function. Call the `accumulate` method on the `add` function:

```
print "Accumulate", np.add.accumulate(a)
```

The accumulated array:

```
Accumulate [ 0  1  3  6 10 15 21 28 36]
```

3. The `reduceat` method is a bit complicated to explain, so let's call it and go through its algorithm, step-by-step. The `reduceat` method requires as arguments, an input array and a list of indices:

```
print "Reduceat", np.add.reduceat(a, [0, 5, 2, 7])
```

The result is shown as follows:

```
Reduceat [10  5 20 15]
```

The first step concerns the indices 0 and 5. This step results in a reduce operation of the array elements between indices 0 and 5.

```
print "Reduceat step I", np.add.reduce(a[0:5])
```

The output of step 1 is as follows:

```
Reduceat step I 10
```

The second step concerns indices 5 and 2. Since 2 is less than 5, the array element at index 5 is returned:

```
print "Reduceat step II", a[5]
```

The second step results in the following output:

```
Reduceat step II 5
```

The third step concerns indices 2 and 7. This step results in a reduce operation of the array elements between indices 2 and 7:

```
print "Reduceat step III", np.add.reduce(a[2:7])
```

The result of the third step is shown as follows:

```
Reduceat step III 20
```

The fourth step concerns index 7. This step results in a reduce operation of the array elements from index 7 to the end of the array:

```
print "Reduceat step IV", np.add.reduce(a[7:])
```

The fourth step result is shown as follows:

```
Reduceat step IV 15
```

4. The `outer` method returns an array that has a rank, which is the sum of the ranks of its two input arrays. The method is applied to all possible pairs of the input array elements. Call the `outer` method on the `add` function:

```
print "Outer", np.add.outer(np.arange(3), a)
```

The outer sum output result is as follows:

```
Outer [[ 0  1  2  3  4  5  6  7  8]
       [ 1  2  3  4  5  6  7  8  9]
       [ 2  3  4  5  6  7  8  9 10]]
```

What just happened?

We applied the four methods, `reduce`, `accumulate`, `reduceat`, and `outer`, of universal functions to the `add` function (see `ufuncmethods.py`):

```
import numpy as np

a = np.arange(9)

print "Reduce", np.add.reduce(a)
print "Accumulate", np.add.accumulate(a)
print "Reduceat", np.add.reduceat(a, [0, 5, 2, 7])
print "Reduceat step I", np.add.reduce(a[0:5])
print "Reduceat step II", a[5]
print "Reduceat step III", np.add.reduce(a[2:7])
print "Reduceat step IV", np.add.reduce(a[7:])
print "Outer", np.add.outer(np.arange(3), a)
```

Arithmetic functions

The common arithmetic operators +, -, and * are implicitly linked to the `add`, `subtract`, and `multiply` universal functions. This means that when you use one of those operators on a NumPy array, the corresponding universal function will get called. Division involves a slightly more complex process. There are three universal functions that have to do with array division: `divide`, `true_divide`, and `floor_division`. Two operators correspond to division: / and //.

Time for action – dividing arrays

Let's see the array division in action:

1. The `divide` function does truncate integer division and normal floating-point division:

```
a = np.array([2, 6, 5])
b = np.array([1, 2, 3])
print "Divide", np.divide(a, b), np.divide(b, a)
```

The result of the `divide` function is shown as follows:

```
Divide [2 3 1] [0 0 0]
```

As you can see, truncation took place.

2. The `true_divide` function comes closer to the mathematical definition of division. Integer division returns a floating-point result and no truncation occurs:

```
print "True Divide", np.true_divide(a, b), np.true_divide(b, a)
```

The result of the `true_divide` function is as follows:

```
True Divide [ 2.          3.          1.66666667] [ 0.5
0.33333333  0.6       ]
```

3. The `floor_divide` function always returns an integer result. It is equivalent to calling the `floor` function after calling the `divide` function. The `floor` function discards the decimal part of a floating-point number and returns an integer:

```
print "Floor Divide", np.floor_divide(a, b), np.floor_divide(b, a)
c = 3.14 * b
print "Floor Divide 2", np.floor_divide(c, b), np.floor_divide(b, c)
```

The `floor_divide` function results in:

```
Floor Divide [2 3 1] [0 0 0]
Floor Divide 2 [ 3.   3.   3.] [ 0.   0.   0.]
```

4. By default, the `/` operator is equivalent to calling the `divide` function:

```
from __future__ import division
```

However, if this line is found at the beginning of a Python program, the `true_divide` function is called instead. So, this code would appear as follows:

```
print "/ operator", a/b, b/a
```

The result is shown as follows:

```
/ operator [ 2.          3.          1.66666667] [ 0.5
0.33333333  0.6        ]
```

5. The // operator is equivalent to calling the `floor_divide` function. For example, look at the following code snippet:

```
print "// operator", a//b, b//a
print "// operator 2", c//b, b//c
```

The // operator result is shown as follows:

```
// operator [2 3 1] [0 0 0]
// operator 2 [ 3.   3.   3.] [ 0.   0.   0.]
```

What just happened?

We found that there are three different NumPy division functions. The `divide` function truncates the integer division and normal floating-point division. The `true_divide` function always returns a floating-point result without any truncation. The `floor_divide` function always returns an integer result; the result is the same that you would get by calling the `divide` and `floor` functions consecutively (see `dividing.py`):

```
from __future__ import division
import numpy as np

a = np.array([2, 6, 5])
b = np.array([1, 2, 3])

print "Divide", np.divide(a, b), np.divide(b, a)
print "True Divide", np.true_divide(a, b), np.true_divide(b, a)
print "Floor Divide", np.floor_divide(a, b), np.floor_divide(b, a)
c = 3.14 * b
print "Floor Divide 2", np.floor_divide(c, b), np.floor_divide(b, c)
print "/ operator", a/b, b/a
print "// operator", a//b, b//a
print "// operator 2", c//b, b//c
```

Have a go hero – experimenting with __future__.division

Experiment to confirm the impact of importing __future__.division.

Modulo operation

The modulo or remainder can be calculated using the NumPy mod, remainder, and fmod functions. Also, one can use the % operator. The main difference among these functions is how they deal with negative numbers. The odd one out in this group is the fmod function.

Time for action – computing the modulo

Let's call the previously mentioned functions:

1. The remainder function returns the remainder of the two arrays, element-wise. 0 is returned if the second number is 0:

   ```
   a = np.arange(-4, 4)
   print "Remainder", np.remainder(a, 2)
   ```

   The result of the remainder function is shown as follows:

   Remainder [0 1 0 1 0 1 0 1]

2. The mod function does exactly the same as the remainder function:

   ```
   print "Mod", np.mod(a, 2)
   ```

   The result of the mod function is shown as follows:

   Mod [0 1 0 1 0 1 0 1]

3. The % operator is just shorthand for the remainder function:

   ```
   print "% operator", a % 2
   ```

   The result of the % operator is shown as follows:

   % operator [0 1 0 1 0 1 0 1]

4. The fmod function handles negative numbers differently than mod, fmod, and % do. The sign of the remainder is the sign of the dividend, and the sign of the divisor has no influence on the results:

   ```
   print "Fmod", np.fmod(a, 2)
   ```

   The fmod result is printed as follows:

   Fmod [0 -1 0 -1 0 1 0 1]

What just happened?

We demonstrated the NumPy `mod`, `remainder`, and `fmod` functions, which compute the modulo, or remainder (see `modulo.py`):

```
import numpy as np

a = np.arange(-4, 4)

print "Remainder", np.remainder(a, 2)
print "Mod", np.mod(a, 2)
print "% operator", a % 2
print "Fmod", np.fmod(a, 2)
```

Fibonacci numbers

The Fibonacci numbers are based on a recurrence relation. It is difficult to express this relation directly with NumPy code. However, we can express this relation in a matrix form or use the golden ratio formula. This will introduce the `matrix` and `rint` functions. The `matrix` function creates matrices and the `rint` function rounds numbers to the closest integer, but the result is not integer.

Time for action – computing Fibonacci numbers

The Fibonacci recurrence relation can be represented by a matrix. Calculation of Fibonacci numbers can be expressed as repeated matrix multiplication:

1. Create the Fibonacci matrix as follows:
   ```
   F = np.matrix([[1, 1], [1, 0]])
   print "F", F
   ```

   The Fibonacci matrix appears as follows:

   ```
   F [[1 1]
      [1 0]]
   ```

2. Calculate the eighth Fibonacci number (ignoring 0), by subtracting 1 from 8 and taking the power of the matrix. The Fibonacci number then appears on the diagonal:
   ```
   print "8th Fibonacci", (F ** 7)[0, 0]
   ```

   The Fibonacci number is:

   ```
   8th Fibonacci 21
   ```

3. The golden ratio formula, better known as Binet's formula, allows us to calculate Fibonacci numbers with a rounding step at the end. Calculate the first eight Fibonacci numbers:

```
n = np.arange(1, 9)
sqrt5 = np.sqrt(5)
phi = (1 + sqrt5)/2
fibonacci = np.rint((phi**n - (-1/phi)**n)/sqrt5)
print "Fibonacci", fibonacci
```

The Fibonacci numbers are:

```
Fibonacci [  1.   1.   2.   3.   5.   8.  13.  21.]
```

What just happened?

We computed Fibonacci numbers in two ways. In the process, we learned about the `matrix` function that creates matrices. We also learned about the `rint` function that rounds numbers to the closest integer but does not change the type to integer (see `fibonacci.py`):

```
import numpy as np

F = np.matrix([[1, 1], [1, 0]])
print "F", F
print "8th Fibonacci", (F ** 7)[0, 0]
n = np.arange(1, 9)

sqrt5 = np.sqrt(5)
phi = (1 + sqrt5)/2
fibonacci = np.rint((phi**n - (-1/phi)**n)/sqrt5)
print "Fibonacci", fibonacci
```

Have a go hero – timing the calculations

You are probably wondering which approach is faster; so go ahead time it. Create a universal Fibonacci function with `frompyfunc` and time it too.

Lissajous curves

All the standard trigonometric functions, such as, sin, cos, tan and likewise are represented by universal functions in NumPy. Lissajous curves are a fun way of using trigonometry. I remember producing Lissajous figures on an oscilloscope in the physics lab. Two parametric equations can describe the figures:

```
x = A sin(at + π/2)
y = B sin(bt)
```

Time for action – drawing Lissajous curves

The Lissajous figures are determined by four parameters A, B, a, and b. Let's set A and B to 1 for simplicity:

1. Initialize t with the `linspace` function from `-pi` to `pi` with `201` points:

   ```
   a = float(sys.argv[1])
   b = float(sys.argv[2])
   t = np.linspace(-np.pi, np.pi, 201)
   ```

2. Calculate x with the `sin` function and `np.pi`:

   ```
   x = np.sin(a * t + np.pi/2)
   ```

3. Calculate y with the `sin` function:

   ```
   y = np.sin(b * t)
   ```

4. `Matplotlib` will be covered later in *Chapter 9, Plotting with Matplotlib*. Plot as shown here:

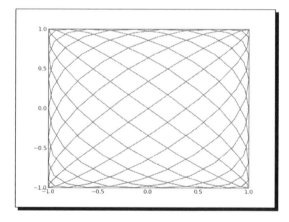

   ```
   plot(x, y)
   show()
   ```

   The result for a = 9 and b = 8 :

What just happened?

We plotted the Lissajous curve with the previously mentioned parametric equations where A=B=1, a=9, and, b=8. We used the `sin` and `linspace` functions as well as the NumPy pi constant (see `lissajous.py`):

```
import numpy as np
from matplotlib.pyplot import plot
from matplotlib.pyplot import show
import sys

a = float(sys.argv[1])
b = float(sys.argv[2])
t = np.linspace(-np.pi, np.pi, 201)
x = np.sin(a * t + np.pi/2)
y = np.sin(b * t)
plot(x, y)
show()
```

Square waves

Square waves are also one of those neat things that you can view on an oscilloscope. They can be approximated pretty well with sine waves; after all, a square wave is a signal that can be represented by an infinite Fourier series.

 A Fourier series is the sum of a series of sine and cosine terms named after the famous mathematician Jean-Baptiste Fourier.

The formula of this particular series representing the square wave is as follows:

$$\sum_{k=1}^{\infty} \frac{4\sin((2k-1)t)}{(2k-1)\pi}$$

Time for action – drawing a square wave

We will initialize t just like in the previous tutorial. We need to sum a number of terms. The higher the number of terms, the more accurate the result; k = 99 should be sufficient. In order to draw a square wave, follow these steps:

1. We will start by initializing t and k. Set initial values for the function to 0:

    ```
    t = np.linspace(-np.pi, np.pi, 201)
    k = np.arange(1, float(sys.argv[1]))
    k = 2 * k - 1
    f = np.zeros_like(t)
    ```

2. This step should be a straightforward application of the `sin` and `sum` functions:

```
for i in range(len(t)):
    f[i] = np.sum(np.sin(k * t[i])/k)
f = (4 / np.pi) * f
```

3. The code to plot is almost identical to the one in the previous tutorial:

```
plot(t, f)
show()
```

The resulting square wave generated with `k = 99` is as follows:

What just happened?

We generated a square wave or, at least, a fair approximation of it, using the `sin` function. The input values were assembled with `linspace` and the `k` values with the `arange` function (see `squarewave.py`):

```
import numpy as np
from matplotlib.pyplot import plot
from matplotlib.pyplot import show
import sys

t = np.linspace(-np.pi, np.pi, 201)
k = np.arange(1, float(sys.argv[1]))
k = 2 * k - 1
f = np.zeros_like(t)

for i in range(len(t)):
```

```
    f[i] = np.sum(np.sin(k * t[i])/k)

f = (4 / np.pi) * f
plot(t, f)
show()
```

Have a go hero – getting rid of the loop

You may have noticed that there is one loop in the code. Get rid of it with NumPy functions and make sure the performance is also improved.

Sawtooth and triangle waves

Sawtooth and triangle waves are also a phenomenon easily viewed on an oscilloscope. Just like with square waves, we can define an infinite Fourier series. The triangle waves can be found by taking the absolute value of a sawtooth wave. The formula for the representation of a series of sawtooth waves is:

$$\sum_{k=1}^{\infty} \frac{-2\sin(2\pi k t)}{k\pi}$$

Time for action – drawing sawtooth and triangle waves

We will initialize t just like in the previous tutorial. Again, k = 99 should be sufficient. In order to draw sawtooth and triangle waves, follow these steps:

1. Set initial values for the function to zero:

   ```
   t = np.linspace(-ny.pi, np.pi, 201)
   k = np.arange(1, float(sys.argv[1]))
   f = np.zeros_like(t)
   ```

2. This computation of function values should again be a straightforward application for the sin and sum functions:

   ```
   for i in range(len(t)):
       f[i] = np.sum(np.sin(2 * np.pi * k * t[i])/k)
   f = (-2 / np.pi) * f
   ```

3. It's easy to plot the sawtooth and triangle waves, since the value of the triangle wave should be equal to the absolute value of the sawtooth wave. Plot the waves as shown here:

```
plot(t, f, lw=1.0)
plot(t, np.abs(f), lw=2.0)
show()
```

In the following figure, the triangle wave is the one with the thicker line:

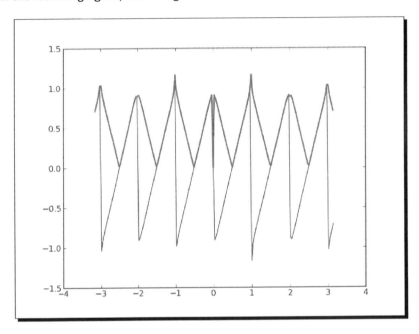

What just happened?

We drew a sawtooth wave using the `sin` function. The input values were assembled with `linspace` and the k values with the `arange` function. A triangle wave was derived from the sawtooth wave by taking the absolute value (see `sawtooth.py`):

```
import numpy as np
from matplotlib.pyplot import plot
from matplotlib.pyplot import show
import sys

t = np.linspace(-np.pi, np.pi, 201)
k = np.arange(1, float(sys.argv[1]))
f = np.zeros_like(t)

for i in range(len(t)):
    f[i] = np.sum(np.sin(2 * np.pi * k * t[i])/k)
```

```
f = (-2 / np.pi) * f
plot(t, f, lw=1.0)
plot(t, np.abs(f), lw=2.0)
show()
```

Have a go hero – getting rid of the loop

Your challenge, should you choose to accept it, is to get rid of the loop in the program. It should be doable with NumPy functions and the performance should double.

Bitwise and comparison functions

Bitwise functions operate on the bits of integers or integer arrays, since they are universal functions. The operators ^, &, |, <<, >>, and so on, have their NumPy counterparts. The same goes for comparison operators, such as, <, >, ==, and likewise. These operators allow you to do some clever tricks, which should be good for performance; however, they could make your code quite unreadable, so use them with care.

Time for action – twiddling bits

We will go over three tricks—checking whether the signs of integers are different, checking whether a number is a power of two, and calculating the modulus of a number that is a power of two. We will show an operators-only notation and one using the corresponding NumPy functions:

1. The first trick depends on the XOR or ^ operator. The XOR operator is also called the inequality operator; so, if the sign bit of the two operands is different, the XOR operation will lead to a negative number. ^ corresponds to the `bitwise_xor` function. < corresponds to the `less` function.

   ```
   x = np.arange(-9, 9)
   y = -x
   print "Sign different?", (x ^ y) < 0
   print "Sign different?", np.less(np.bitwise_xor(x, y), 0)
   ```

   The result is shown as follows:

   ```
   Sign different? [ True  True  True  True  True  True  True  True
   True False  True  True
     True  True  True  True  True  True]
   Sign different? [ True  True  True  True  True  True  True  True
   True False  True  True
     True  True  True  True  True  True]
   ```

   As expected, all the signs differ, except for zero.

2. A power of two is represented by a 1, followed by a series of trailing zeroes in binary notation. For instance, `10`, `100`, or `1000`. A number one less than a power of two would be represented by a row of ones in binary. For instance, `11`, `111`, or `1111` (or 3, 7, and 15, in the decimal system). Now, if we bitwise the AND operator a power of two, and the integer that is one less than that, then we should get `0`. The NumPy counterpart of `&` is `bitwise_and`; the counterpart of `==` is the `equal` universal function.

```
print "Power of 2?\n", x, "\n", (x & (x - 1)) == 0
print "Power of 2?\n", x, "\n", np.equal(np.bitwise_and(x,
   (x - 1)), 0)
```

The result is shown as follows:

```
Power of 2?
[-9 -8 -7 -6 -5 -4 -3 -2 -1  0  1  2  3  4  5  6  7  8]
[False False False False False False False False False  True  True
True
 False  True False False False  True]
Power of 2?
[-9 -8 -7 -6 -5 -4 -3 -2 -1  0  1  2  3  4  5  6  7  8]
[False False False False False False False False False  True  True
True
 False  True False False False  True]
```

3. The trick of computing the modulus of four actually works when taking the modulus of integers that are a power of two, such as, 4, 8, 16, and likewise. A bitwise left shift leads to doubling of values. We saw in the previous step that subtracting one from a power of two leads to a number in binary notation that has a row of ones, such as, `11`, `111`, or `1111`. This basically gives us a mask. Bitwise-ANDing with such a number gives you the remainder with a power of two. The NumPy equivalent of `<<` is the `left_shift` universal function.

```
print "Modulus 4\n", x, "\n", x & ((1 << 2) - 1)
print "Modulus 4\n", x, "\n", np.bitwise_and(x,
   np.left_shift(1, 2) - 1)
```

The result is shown as follows:

```
Modulus 4
[-9 -8 -7 -6 -5 -4 -3 -2 -1  0  1  2  3  4  5  6  7  8]
[3 0 1 2 3 0 1 2 3 0 1 2 3 0 1 2 3 0]
Modulus 4
[-9 -8 -7 -6 -5 -4 -3 -2 -1  0  1  2  3  4  5  6  7  8]
[3 0 1 2 3 0 1 2 3 0 1 2 3 0 1 2 3 0]
```

What just happened?

We covered three bit-twiddling hacks—checking whether the signs of integers are different, checking whether a number is a power of two, and calculating the modulus of a number that is a power of two. We saw the NumPy counterparts of the operators ^, &, <<, and < (see `bittwidling.py`):

```
import numpy as np

x = np.arange(-9, 9)
y = -x
print "Sign different?", (x ^ y) < 0
print "Sign different?", np.less(np.bitwise_xor(x, y), 0)
print "Power of 2?\n", x, "\n", (x & (x - 1)) == 0
print "Power of 2?\n", x, "\n", np.equal(np.bitwise_and(x,  (x - 1)),
0)
print "Modulus 4\n", x, "\n", x & ((1 << 2) - 1)
print "Modulus 4\n", x, "\n", np.bitwise_and(x, np.left_shift(1, 2) -
1)
```

Summary

We learned, in this chapter, about matrices and universal functions. We covered how to create matrices and how universal functions work. We had a brief introduction to arithmetic, trigonometric, bitwise, and comparison universal functions.

In the next chapter, we shall cover the NumPy modules.

6 Move Further with NumPy Modules

NumPy has a number of modules that have been inherited from its predecessor, Numeric. Some of these packages have a SciPy counterpart, which may have fuller functionality. This will be discussed in a later chapter. The `numpy.dual` *package contains functions that are defined both in NumPy and SciPy. The packages discussed in this chapter are also part of the* `numpy.dual` *package.*

In this chapter, we shall cover the following topics:

- ◆ The `linalg` package
- ◆ The `fft` package
- ◆ Random numbers
- ◆ Continuous and discrete distributions

Linear algebra

Linear algebra is an important branch of mathematics. The `numpy.linalg` package contains linear algebra functions. With this module, you can invert matrices, calculate eigenvalues, solve linear equations, and determine determinants, among other things.

Time for action – inverting matrices

The inverse of a matrix `A` in linear algebra is the matrix `A`$^{-1}$, which when multiplied with the original matrix, is equal to the identity matrix I. This can be written, as $A * A^{-1} = I$.

The `inv` function in the `numpy.linalg` package can do this for us. Let's invert an example matrix. To invert matrices, perform the following steps:

1. We will create the example matrix with the `mat` function that we used in the previous chapters.

```
A = np.mat("0 1 2;1 0 3;4 -3 8")
print "A\n", A
```

The A matrix is printed as follows:

```
A
[[ 0  1  2]
 [ 1  0  3]
 [ 4 -3  8]]
```

2. Now, we can see the `inv` function in action, using which we will invert the matrix.

```
inverse = np.linalg.inv(A)
print "inverse of A\n", inverse
```

The inverse matrix is shown as follows:

```
inverse of A
[[-4.5  7.  -1.5]
 [-2.   4.  -1. ]
 [ 1.5 -2.   0.5]]
```

 If the matrix is singular or not square, a `LinAlgError` exception is raised. If you want, you can check the result manually. This is left as an exercise for the reader.

3. Let's check what we get when we multiply the original matrix with the result of the `inv` function:

```
print "Check\n", A * inverse
```

The result is the identity matrix, as expected.

```
Check
[[ 1.  0.  0.]
 [ 0.  1.  0.]
 [ 0.  0.  1.]]
```

What just happened?

We calculated the inverse of a matrix with the `inv` function of the `numpy.linalg` package. We checked, with matrix multiplication, whether this is indeed the inverse matrix (see `inversion.py`).

```
import numpy as np

A = np.mat("0 1 2;1 0 3;4 -3 8")
print "A\n", A

inverse = np.linalg.inv(A)
print "inverse of A\n", inverse

print "Check\n", A * inverse
```

Pop quiz – creating a matrix

Q1. Which function can create matrices?

1. `array`
2. `create_matrix`
3. `mat`
4. `vector`

Have a go hero – inverting your own matrix

Create your own matrix and invert it. The inverse is only defined for square matrices. The matrix must be square and invertible; otherwise, a `LinAlgError` exception is raised.

Solving linear systems

A matrix transforms a vector into another vector in a linear way. This transformation mathematically corresponds to a system of linear equations. The `numpy.linalg` function, `solve`, solves systems of linear equations of the form $Ax = b$; here A is a matrix, b can be 1D or 2D array, and x is an unknown variable. We will see the `dot` function in action. This function returns the dot product of two floating-point arrays.

Time for action – solving a linear system

Let's solve an example of a linear system. To solve a linear system, perform the following steps:

1. Let's create the matrices A and b.

```
A = np.mat("1 -2 1;0 2 -8;-4 5 9")
print "A\n", A
b = np.array([0, 8, -9])
print "b\n", b
```

The matrices A and b are shown as follows:

```
A
[[ 1  -2   1]
 [ 0   2  -8]
 [-4   5   9]]
b
[ 0   8  -9]
```

2. Solve this linear system by calling the solve function.

```
x = np.linalg.solve(A, b)
print "Solution", x
```

The following is the solution of the linear system:

```
Solution [ 29.  16.   3.]
```

3. Check whether the solution is correct with the dot function.

```
print "Check\n", np.dot(A , x)
```

The result is as expected:

```
Check
[[ 0.  8. -9.]]
```

What just happened?

We solved a linear system using the solve function from the NumPy linalg module and checked the solution with the dot function (see solution.py).

```
import numpy as np

A = np.mat("1 -2 1;0 2 -8;-4 5 9")
print "A\n", A

b = np.array([0, 8, -9])
```

```
print "b\n", b

x = np.linalg.solve(A, b)
print "Solution", x

print "Check\n", np.dot(A , x)
```

Finding eigenvalues and eigenvectors

Eigenvalues are scalar solutions to the equation *Ax = ax*, where *A* is a two-dimensional matrix and *x* is a one-dimensional vector. **Eigenvectors** are vectors corresponding to eigenvalues. The `eigvals` function in the `numpy.linalg` package calculates eigenvalues. The `eig` function returns a tuple containing eigenvalues and eigenvectors.

Time for action – determining eigenvalues and eigenvectors

Let's calculate the eigenvalues of a matrix. Perform the following steps to do so:

1. Create a matrix as follows:

   ```
   A = np.mat("3 -2;1 0")
   print "A\n", A
   ```

   The matrix we created looks like the following:

   ```
   A
   [[ 3 -2]
    [ 1  0]]
   ```

2. Calculate eigenvalues by calling the `eig` function.

   ```
   print "Eigenvalues", np.linalg.eigvals(A)
   ```

   The eigenvalues of the matrix are as follows:

   ```
   Eigenvalues [ 2.  1.]
   ```

3. Determine eigenvalues and eigenvectors with the `eig` function. This function returns a tuple, where the first element contains eigenvalues and the second element contains corresponding Eigenvectors, arranged column-wise.

   ```
   eigenvalues, eigenvectors = np.linalg.eig(A)
   print "First tuple of eig", eigenvalues
   print "Second tuple of eig\n", eigenvectors
   ```

The eigenvalues and eigenvectors will be shown as follows:

```
First tuple of eig [ 2.   1.]
Second tuple of eig
[[ 0.89442719  0.70710678]
 [ 0.4472136   0.70710678]]
```

4. Check the result with the `dot` function by calculating the right- and left-hand sides of the `eigenvalues` equation $Ax = ax$.

```
for i in range(len(eigenvalues)):
    print "Left", np.dot(A, eigenvectors[:,i])
    print "Right", eigenvalues[i] * eigenvectors[:,i]
    print
```

The output is as follows:

```
Left [[ 1.78885438]
 [ 0.89442719]]
Right [[ 1.78885438]
 [ 0.89442719]]
Left [[ 0.70710678]
 [ 0.70710678]]
Right [[ 0.70710678]
 [ 0.70710678]]
```

What just happened?

We found the eigenvalues and eigenvectors of a matrix with the `eigvals` and `eig` functions of the `numpy.linalg` module. We checked the result using the `dot` function (see `eigenvalues.py`).

```
import numpy as np

A = np.mat("3 -2;1 0")
print "A\n", A

print "Eigenvalues", np.linalg.eigvals(A)

eigenvalues, eigenvectors = np.linalg.eig(A)
print "First tuple of eig", eigenvalues
print "Second tuple of eig\n", eigenvectors

for i in range(len(eigenvalues)):
    print "Left", np.dot(A, eigenvectors[:,i])
    print "Right", eigenvalues[i] * eigenvectors[:,i]
    print
```

Singular value decomposition

Singular value decomposition is a type of factorization that decomposes a matrix into a product of three matrices. The singular value decomposition is a generalization of the previously discussed eigenvalue decomposition. The `svd` function in the `numpy.linalg` package can perform this decomposition. This function returns three matrices – *U*, Sigma, and *V* – such that *U* and *V* are orthogonal and Sigma contains the singular values of the input matrix.

The asterisk denotes the Hermitian conjugate or the conjugate transpose.

Time for action – decomposing a matrix

It's time to decompose a matrix with the singular value decomposition. In order to decompose a matrix, perform the following steps:

1. First, create a matrix as follows:

    ```
    A = np.mat("4 11 14;8 7 -2")
    print "A\n", A
    ```

    The matrix we created looks like the following:

    ```
    A
    [[ 4 11 14]
     [ 8  7 -2]]
    ```

2. Decompose the matrix with the `svd` function.

    ```
    U, Sigma, V = np.linalg.svd(A, full_matrices=False)
    print "U"
    print U
    print "Sigma"
    print Sigma
    print "V"
    print V
    ```

    The result is a tuple containing the two orthogonal matrices `U` and `V` on the left- and right-hand sides and the singular values of the middle matrix.

    ```
    U
    [[-0.9486833  -0.31622777]
     [-0.31622777  0.9486833 ]]
    ```

```
Sigma
[ 18.97366596    9.48683298]
V
[[-0.33333333 -0.66666667 -0.66666667]
 [ 0.66666667  0.33333333 -0.66666667]]
```

3. We do not actually have the middle matrix—we only have the diagonal values. The other values are all 0. We can form the middle matrix with the `diag` function. Multiply the three matrices. This is shown, as follows:

```
print "Product\n", U * np.diag(Sigma) * V
```

The product of the three matrices looks like the following:

```
Product
[[  4.  11.  14.]
 [  8.   7.  -2.]]
```

What just happened?

We decomposed a matrix and checked the result by matrix multiplication. We used the `svd` function from the NumPy `linalg` module (see `decomposition.py`).

```
import numpy as np

A = np.mat("4 11 14;8 7 -2")
print "A\n", A

U, Sigma, V = np.linalg.svd(A, full_matrices=False)

print "U"
print U

print "Sigma"
print Sigma

print "V"
print V

print "Product\n", U * np.diag(Sigma) * V
```

Pseudoinverse

The Moore-Penrose pseudoinverse of a matrix can be computed with the `pinv`
function of the `numpy.linalg` module (visit `http://en.wikipedia.org/wiki/`
`Moore%E2%80%93Penrose_pseudoinverse`). The pseudoinverse is calculated using the
singular value decomposition. The `inv` function only accepts square matrices; the `pinv`
function does not have this restriction.

Time for action – computing the pseudo inverse of a matrix

Let's compute the pseudo inverse of a matrix. Perform the following steps to do so:

1. First, create a matrix as follows:

```
A = np.mat("4 11 14;8 7 -2")
print "A\n", A
```

The matrix we created looks like the following:

```
A
[[ 4 11 14]
 [ 8  7 -2]]
```

2. Calculate the pseudoinverse matrix with the `pinv` function, as follows:

```
pseudoinv = np.linalg.pinv(A)
print "Pseudo inverse\n", pseudoinv
```

The following is the pseudoinverse:

```
Pseudo inverse
[[-0.00555556  0.07222222]
 [ 0.02222222  0.04444444]
 [ 0.05555556 -0.05555556]]
```

3. Multiply the original and pseudoinverse matrices.

```
print "Check", A * pseudoinv
```

What we get is not an identity matrix, but it comes close to it, as follows:

```
Check [[  1.00000000e+00   0.00000000e+00]
 [  8.32667268e-17   1.00000000e+00]]
```

What just happened?

We computed the pseudoinverse of a matrix with the `pinv` function of the `numpy.linalg` module. The check by matrix multiplication resulted in a matrix that is approximately an identity matrix (see `pseudoinversion.py`).

```
import numpy as np

A = np.mat("4 11 14;8 7 -2")
print "A\n", A

pseudoinv = np.linalg.pinv(A)
print "Pseudo inverse\n", pseudoinv

print "Check", A * pseudoinv
```

Determinants

The determinant is a value associated with a square matrix. It is used throughout mathematics; for more details please visit `http://en.wikipedia.org/wiki/Determinant`. For an *n x n* real value matrix the determinant corresponds to the scaling an *n*-dimensional volume undergoes when transformed by the matrix. The positive sign of the determinant means the volume preserves its orientation ("clockwise" or "anticlockwise"), while a negative sign means reversed orientation. The `numpy.linalg` module has a `det` function that returns the determinant of a matrix.

Time for action – calculating the determinant of a matrix

To calculate the determinant of a matrix, perform the following steps:

1. Create the matrix as follows:

   ```
   A = np.mat("3 4;5 6")
   print "A\n", A
   ```

   The matrix we created is shown as follows:

   ```
   A
   [[ 3.  4.]
    [ 5.  6.]]
   ```

2. Compute the determinant with the `det` function.

   ```
   print "Determinant", np.linalg.det(A)
   ```

   The determinant is shown as follows:

   ```
   Determinant -2.0
   ```

What just happened?

We calculated the determinant of a matrix with the det function from the numpy.linalg module (see determinant.py).

```
import numpy as np

A = np.mat("3 4;5 6")
print "A\n", A

print "Determinant", np.linalg.det(A)
```

Fast Fourier transform

The **fast Fourier transform (FFT)** is an efficient algorithm to calculate the **discrete Fourier transform (DFT)**. FFT improves on more naïve algorithms and is of order *O(NlogN)*. DFT has applications in signal processing, image processing, solving partial differential equations, and more. NumPy has a module called fft that offers fast Fourier transform functionality. A lot of the functions in this module are paired; this means that, for many functions, there is a function that does the inverse operation. For instance, the fft and ifft functions form such a pair.

Time for action – calculating the Fourier transform

First, we will create a signal to transform. In order to calculate the Fourier transform, perform the following steps:

1. Create a cosine wave with 30 points, as follows:

    ```
    x =  np.linspace(0, 2 * np.pi, 30)
    wave = np.cos(x)
    ```

2. Transform the cosine wave with the fft function.

    ```
    transformed = np.fft.fft(wave)
    ```

3. Apply the inverse transform with the ifft function. It should approximately return the original signal.

    ```
    print np.all(np.abs(np.fft.ifft(transformed) - wave) < 10 ** -9)
    ```

    The result is shown as follows:

    ```
    True
    ```

4. Plot the transformed signal with Matplotlib.

```
plot(transformed)
show()
```

The resulting screenshot shows the fast Fourier transform:

What just happened?

We applied the `fft` function to a cosine wave. After applying the `ifft` function we got our signal back (see `fourier.py`).

```
import numpy as np
from matplotlib.pyplot import plot, show

x =  np.linspace(0, 2 * np.pi, 30)
wave = np.cos(x)
transformed = np.fft.fft(wave)
print np.all(np.abs(np.fft.ifft(transformed) - wave) < 10 ** -9)

plot(transformed)
show()
```

Shifting

The `fftshift` function of the `numpy.linalg` module shifts zero-frequency components to the center of a spectrum. The `ifftshift` function reverses this operation.

Time for action – shifting frequencies

We will create a signal, transform it, and then shift the signal. In order to shift the frequencies, perform the following steps:

1. Create a cosine wave with `30` points.

```
x =  np.linspace(0, 2 * np.pi, 30)
wave = np.cos(x)
```

2. Transform the cosine wave with the `fft` function.

```
transformed = np.fft.fft(wave)
```

3. Shift the signal with the `fftshift` function.

```
shifted = np.fft.fftshift(transformed)
```

4. Reverse the shift with the `ifftshift` function. This should undo the shift.

```
print np.all((np.fft.ifftshift(shifted) - transformed) < 10 ** -9)
```

The result is shown as follows:

```
True
```

5. Plot the signal and transform it with Matplotlib.

```
plot(transformed, lw=2)
plot(shifted, lw=3)
show()
```

The following screenshot shows the shift in the fast Fourier transform:

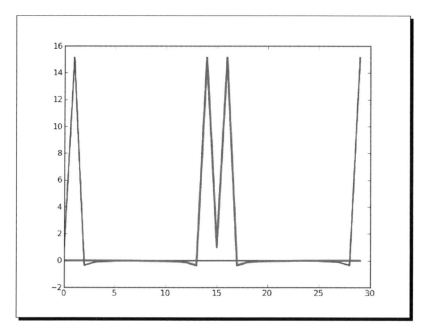

What just happened?

We applied the `fftshift` function to a cosine wave. After applying the `ifftshift` function, we got our signal back (see `fouriershift.py`).

```
import numpy as np
from matplotlib.pyplot import plot, show

x =  np.linspace(0, 2 * np.pi, 30)
wave = np.cos(x)
transformed = np.fft.fft(wave)
shifted = np.fft.fftshift(transformed)
print np.all(np.abs(np.fft.ifftshift(shifted) - transformed) < 10 **
-9)

plot(transformed, lw=2)
plot(shifted, lw=3)
show()
```

Random numbers

Random numbers are used in Monte Carlo methods, stochastic calculus, and more. Real random numbers are hard to generate, so in practice we use pseudo random numbers. Pseudo random numbers are random enough for most intents and purposes, except for some very special cases. The functions related to random numbers can be found in the NumPy `random` module. The core random number generator is based on the Mersenne Twister algorithm. Random numbers can be generated from discrete or continuous distributions. The distribution functions have an optional `size` parameter, which tells NumPy how many numbers to generate. You can specify either an integer or a tuple as size. This will result in an array filled with random numbers of appropriate shape. Discrete distributions include the geometric, hypergeometric, and binomial distributions.

Time for action – gambling with the binomial

The binomial distribution models the number of successes in an integer number of independent trials of an experiment, where the probability of success in each experiment is a fixed number.

Imagine a 17th-century gambling house where you can bet on flipping of pieces of eight. Nine coins are flipped. If less than five are heads, then you lose one piece of eight, otherwise you win one. Let's simulate this, starting with 1000 coins in our possession. We will use the `binomial` function from the `random` module for that purpose.

In order to understand the `binomial` function, go through the following steps:

1. Initialize an array, which represents the cash balance, to zeros. Call the `binomial` function with a size of `10000`. This represents 10,000 coin flips in our casino.

```
cash = np.zeros(10000)
cash[0] = 1000
outcome = np.random.binomial(9, 0.5, size=len(cash))
```

2. Go through the outcomes of the coin flips and update the `cash` array. Print the minimum and maximum of `outcome`, just to make sure we don't have any strange outliers.

```
for i in range(1, len(cash)):
    if outcome[i] < 5:
        cash[i] = cash[i - 1] - 1
    elif outcome[i] < 10:
        cash[i] = cash[i - 1] + 1
    else:
        raise AssertionError("Unexpected outcome " + outcome)
print outcome.min(), outcome.max()
```

As expected, the values are between 0 and 9.

```
0  9
```

3. Plot the `cash` array with Matplotlib.

```
plot(np.arange(len(cash)), cash)
show()
```

As you can see in the following screenshot, our cash balance performs a random walk:

What just happened?

We did a random walk experiment using the `binomial` function from the NumPy random module (see `headortail.py`).

```
import numpy as np
from matplotlib.pyplot import plot, show

cash = np.zeros(10000)
cash[0] = 1000
outcome = np.random.binomial(9, 0.5, size=len(cash))

for i in range(1, len(cash)):
```

```
    if outcome[i] < 5:
      cash[i] = cash[i - 1] - 1
    elif outcome[i] < 10:
      cash[i] = cash[i - 1] + 1
    else:
      raise AssertionError("Unexpected outcome " + outcome)

print outcome.min(), outcome.max()

plot(np.arange(len(cash)), cash)
show()
```

Hypergeometric distribution

The hypergeometric distribution models a jar with two types of objects in it. The model tells us how many objects of one type we can get if we take a specified number of items out of the jar without replacing them. The NumPy random module has a hypergeometric function that simulates this situation.

Time for action – simulating a game show

Imagine a game show where every time the contestants answer a question correctly, they get to pull three balls from a jar and then put them back. Now there is a catch, there is one ball in there that is bad. Every time it is pulled out, the contestants lose six points. If however, they manage to get out three of the 25 normal balls, they get one point. So, what is going to happen if we have 100 questions in total? In order to get a solution for this, go through the following steps:

1. Initialize the outcome of the game with the hypergeometric function. The first parameter of this function is the number of ways to make a good selection, the second parameter is the number of ways to make a bad selection, and the third parameter is the number of items sampled.

```
points = np.zeros(100)
outcomes = np.random.hypergeometric(25, 1, 3, size=len(points))
```

2. Set the scores based on the outcomes from the previous step.

```
for i in range(len(points)):
    if outcomes[i] == 3:
      points[i] = points[i - 1] + 1
    elif outcomes[i] == 2:
      points[i] = points[i - 1] - 6
    else:
      print outcomes[i]
```

3. Plot the `points` array with Matplotlib.

```
plot(np.arange(len(points)), points)
show()
```

The following screenshot shows how the scoring evolved:

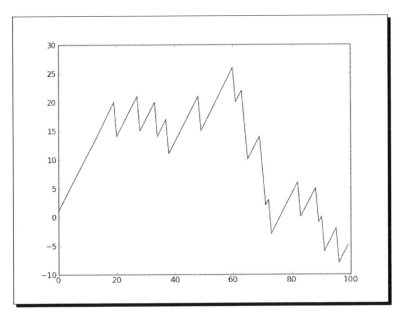

What just happened?

We simulated a game show using the `hypergeometric` function from the NumPy `random` module. The game scoring depends on how many good and how many bad balls are pulled out of a jar in each session (see `urn.py`).

```
import numpy as np
from matplotlib.pyplot import plot, show

points = np.zeros(100)
outcomes = np.random.hypergeometric(25, 1, 3, size=len(points))

for i in range(len(points)):
    if outcomes[i] == 3:
        points[i] = points[i - 1] + 1
    elif outcomes[i] == 2:
        points[i] = points[i - 1] - 6
    else:
        print outcomes[i]
```

```
plot(np.arange(len(points)), points)
show()
```

Continuous distributions

Continuous distributions are modeled by the **probability density functions (pdf)**. The probability for a certain interval is determined by integration of the probability density function. The NumPy `random` module has a number of functions that represent continuous distributions—beta, chisquare, exponential, f, gamma, gumbel, laplace, lognormal, logistic, multivariate_normal, noncentral_chisquare, noncentral_f, normal, and others.

Time for action – drawing a normal distribution

Random numbers can be generated from a normal distribution and their distribution may be visualized with a histogram. To draw a normal distribution, perform the following steps:

1. Generate random numbers for a given sample size using the `normal` function from the `random` NumPy module.

```
N=10000
normal_values = np.random.normal(size=N)
```

2. Draw the histogram and theoretical pdf: Draw the histogram and theoretical pdf with a center value of 0 and standard deviation of 1. We will use Matplotlib for this purpose.

```
dummy, bins, dummy = plt.hist(normal_values,
   np.sqrt(N), normed=True, lw=1)
sigma = 1
mu = 0
plt.plot(bins, 1/(sigma * np.sqrt(2 * np.pi))
   * np.exp( - (bins - mu)**2 / (2 * sigma**2) ),lw=2)
plt.show()
```

In the following screenshot, we see the familiar bell curve:

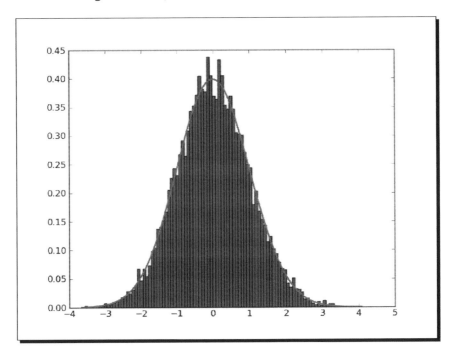

What just happened?

We visualized the normal distribution using the `normal` function from the `random` NumPy module. We did this by drawing the bell curve and a histogram of randomly generated values (see `normaldist.py`).

```
import numpy as np
import matplotlib.pyplot as plt

N=10000

normal_values = np.random.normal(size=N)
dummy, bins, dummy = plt.hist(normal_values, np.sqrt(N), normed=True,
lw=1)
sigma = 1
mu = 0
plt.plot(bins, 1/(sigma * np.sqrt(2 * np.pi)) * np.exp( - (bins -
mu)**2 / (2 * sigma**2) ),lw=2)
plt.show()
```

Lognormal distribution

A **lognormal distribution** is a distribution of a variable whose natural logarithm is normally distributed. The `lognormal` function of the `random` NumPy module models this distribution.

Time for action – drawing the lognormal distribution

Let's visualize the lognormal distribution and its probability density function with a histogram. Perform the following steps:

1. Generate random numbers using the `normal` function from the `random` NumPy module.

```
N=10000
lognormal_values = np.random.lognormal(size=N)
```

2. Draw the histogram and theoretical pdf: Draw the histogram and theoretical pdf with a center value of `0` and standard deviation of `1`. We will use Matplotlib for this purpose.

```
dummy, bins, dummy = plt.hist(lognormal_values,
   np.sqrt(N), normed=True, lw=1)
sigma = 1
mu = 0
x = np.linspace(min(bins), max(bins), len(bins))
pdf = np.exp(-(numpy.log(x) - mu)**2 / (2 * sigma**2))/ (x *
   sigma * np.sqrt(2 * np.pi))
plt.plot(x, pdf,lw=3)
plt.show()
```

The fit of the histogram and theoretical pdf is excellent, as you can see in the following screenshot:

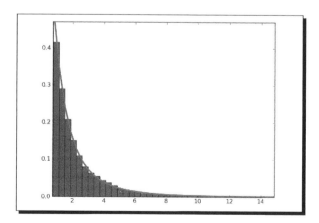

What just happened?

We visualized the lognormal distribution using the `lognormal` function from the `random` NumPy module. We did this by drawing the curve of the theoretical probability density function and a histogram of randomly generated values (see `lognormaldist.py`).

```
import numpy as np
import matplotlib.pyplot as plt

N=10000
lognormal_values = np.random.lognormal(size=N)
dummy, bins, dummy = plt.hist(lognormal_values, np.sqrt(N),
normed=True, lw=1)
sigma = 1
mu = 0
x = np.linspace(min(bins), max(bins), len(bins))
pdf = np.exp(-(np.log(x) - mu)**2 / (2 * sigma**2))/ (x * sigma *
np.sqrt(2 * np.pi))
plt.plot(x, pdf,lw=3)
plt.show()
```

Summary

We learned a lot in this chapter about NumPy modules. We covered linear algebra, the fast Fourier transform, continuous and discrete distributions, and random numbers.

In the next chapter, we shall cover specialized routines. These are functions that you probably would not use often, but are very useful when you do need them.

7
Peeking into Special Routines

As NumPy users, we sometimes find ourselves having special needs for instance financial calculations or signal processing. Fortunately, NumPy provides for most of our needs. This chapter describes some of the more specialized NumPy functions.

In this chapter we will cover the following topics:

- Sorting and searching
- Special functions
- Financial utilities
- Window functions

Sorting

NumPy has several data sorting routines, as follows:

- The `sort` function returns a sorted array
- The `lexsort` function performs sorting with a list of keys
- The `argsort` function returns the indices that would sort an array
- The `ndarray` class has a `sort` method that performs place sorting
- The `msort` function sorts an array along the first axis
- The `sort_complex` function sorts complex numbers by their real part and then their imaginary part

From this list `argsort` and `sort` are available as methods on NumPy arrays as well.

Time for action – sorting lexically

The NumPy `lexsort` function returns an array of indices of the input array elements corresponding to lexically sorting an array. We need to give the function an array or tuple of sort keys. Perform the following steps:

1. Now for something completely different, let's go back to *Chapter 3, Get to Terms with Commonly Used Functions*. In that chapter we used stock price data of AAPL. This is by now pretty old data. We will load the close prices and the always complex dates. In fact, we will need a converter function just for the dates.

```
def datestr2num(s):
    return datetime.datetime.strptime
    (s, "%d-%m-%Y").toordinal()

dates,closes=np.loadtxt('AAPL.csv', delimiter=',',
    usecols=(1, 6), converters={1:datestr2num}, unpack=True)
```

2. Sort the names lexically with the `lexsort` function. The data is already sorted by date, but we will now sort it by close as well.

```
indices = np.lexsort((dates, closes))

print "Indices", indices
print ["%s %s" % (datetime.date.fromordinal(dates[i]),
    closes[i]) for i in indices]
```

The code prints the following:

```
['2011-01-28 336.1', '2011-02-22 338.61', '2011-01-31 339.32',
'2011-02-23 342.62', '2011-02-24 342.88', '2011-02-03 343.44',
'2011-02-02 344.32', '2011-02-01 345.03', '2011-02-04 346.5',
'2011-03-10 346.67', '2011-02-25 348.16', '2011-03-01 349.31',
'2011-02-18 350.56', '2011-02-07 351.88', '2011-03-11 351.99',
'2011-03-02 352.12', '2011-03-09 352.47', '2011-02-28 353.21',
'2011-02-10 354.54', '2011-02-08 355.2', '2011-03-07 355.36',
'2011-03-08 355.76', '2011-02-11 356.85', '2011-02-09 358.16',
'2011-02-17 358.3', '2011-02-14 359.18', '2011-03-03 359.56',
'2011-02-15 359.9', '2011-03-04 360.0', '2011-02-16 363.13']
```

What just happened?

We sorted the close prices of AAPL lexically using the NumPy `lexsort` function. The function returned the indices corresponding with sorting the array (see `lex.py`).

```
import numpy as np
import datetime
```

```
def datestr2num(s):
    return datetime.datetime.strptime(s, "%d-%m-%Y").toordinal()

dates,closes=np.loadtxt('AAPL.csv', delimiter=',', usecols=(1, 6),
converters={1:datestr2num}, unpack=True)
indices = np.lexsort((dates, closes))

print "Indices", indices
print ["%s %s" % (datetime.date.fromordinal(int(dates[i])),
closes[i]) for i in indices]
```

Have a go hero – trying a different sort order

We sorted using the dates, close price sort order. Try a different order. Generate random numbers using the `random` module we learned about in the previous chapter and sort those using `lexsort`.

Complex numbers

Complex numbers are numbers that have a real and imaginary part. As you remember from previous chapters, NumPy has special complex data types that represent complex numbers by two floating point numbers. These numbers can be sorted using the NumPy `sort_complex` function. This function sorts the real part first and then the imaginary part.

Time for action – sorting complex numbers

We will create an array of complex numbers and sort it. Perform the following steps to do so:

1. Generate five random numbers for the real part of the complex numbers and five numbers for the imaginary part. Seed the random generator to 42.

    ```
    np.random.seed(42)
    complex_numbers = np.random.random(5) + 1j * np.random.random(5)
    print "Complex numbers\n", complex_numbers
    ```

2. Call the `sort_complex` function to sort the complex numbers we generated in the previous step.

    ```
    print "Sorted\n", np.sort_complex(complex_numbers)
    ```

    The sorted numbers would be shown as follows:

    ```
    Sorted
    [ 0.39342751+0.34955771j   0.40597665+0.77477433j
    0.41516850+0.26221878j
      0.86631422+0.74612422j   0.92293095+0.81335691j]
    ```

What just happened?

We generated random complex numbers and sorted them using the `sort_complex` function (see `sortcomplex.py`).

```
import numpy as np

np.random.seed(42)
complex_numbers = np.random.random(5) + 1j * np.random.random(5)
print "Complex numbers\n", complex_numbers

print "Sorted\n", np.sort_complex(complex_numbers)
```

Pop quiz – generating random numbers

Q1. Which NumPy module deals with random numbers?

1. `Randnum`
2. `random`
3. `randomutil`
4. `rand`

Searching

NumPy has several functions that can search through arrays, as follows:

◆ The `argmax` function gives the indices of the maximum values of an array.

```
>>> a = np.array([2, 4, 8])
>>> np.argmax(a)
2
```

◆ The `nanargmax` function does the same but ignores NaN values.

```
>>> b = np.array([np.nan, 2, 4])
>>> np.nanargmax(b)
2
```

◆ The `argmin` and `nanargmin` functions provide similar functionality but pertaining to minimum values.

◆ The `argwhere` function searches for non-zero values and returns the corresponding indices grouped by element.

```
>>> a = np.array([2, 4, 8])
>>> np.argwhere(a <= 4)
array([[0],
       [1]])
```

◆ The `searchsorted` function tells you the index in an array where a specified value could be inserted to maintain the sort order. It uses binary search, which is a *O(log n)* algorithm. We will see this function in action shortly.

◆ The `extract` function retrieves values from an array based on a condition.

Time for action – using searchsorted

The `searchsorted` function allows us to get the index of a value in a sorted array, where it could be inserted so that the array remains sorted. An example should make this clear. Perform the following steps:

1. To demonstrate we will need an array that is sorted. Create an array with `arange`, which of course is sorted.

   ```
   a = np.arange(5)
   ```

2. It's time to call the `searchsorted` function.

   ```
   indices = np.searchsorted(a, [-2, 7])
   print "Indices", indices
   ```

   The following are the indices which should maintain the sort order:

   ```
   Indices [0 5]
   ```

3. Let's construct the full array with the `insert` function.

   ```
   print "The full array", np.insert(a, indices, [-2, 7])
   ```

   This gives us the full array:

   ```
   The full array [-2  0  1  2  3  4  7]
   ```

What just happened?

The `searchsorted` function gave us indices 5 and 0 for 7 and -2. With these indices, we would make the array `[-2, 0, 1, 2, 3, 4, 7]`—so the array remains sorted (see `sortedsearch.py`).

```
import numpy as np

a = np.arange(5)
indices = np.searchsorted(a, [-2, 7])
print "Indices", indices

print "The full array", np.insert(a, indices, [-2, 7])
```

Array elements' extraction

The NumPy `extract` function allows us to extract items from an array based on a condition. This function is similar to the `where` function we encountered in *Chapter 3, Get to Terms with Commonly Used Functions*. The special `nonzero` function selects non-zero elements.

Time for action – extracting elements from an array

Let's extract the even elements from an array. Perform the following steps to do so:

1. Create the array with the `arange` function.

    ```
    a = np.arange(7)
    ```

2. Create the condition that selects the even elements.

    ```
    condition = (a % 2) == 0
    ```

3. Extract the even elements based on our condition with the `extract` function.

    ```
    print "Even numbers", np.extract(condition, a)
    ```

    This gives us the even numbers, as required:

    Even numbers [0 2 4 6]

4. Select non-zero values with the `nonzero` function.

    ```
    print "Non zero", np.nonzero(a)
    ```

    This prints all the non-zero values of the array, as follows:

    Non zero (array([1, 2, 3, 4, 5, 6]),)

What just happened?

We extracted the even elements from an array based on a Boolean condition with the NumPy `extract` function (see `extracted.py`).

```
import numpy as np

a = np.arange(7)
condition = (a % 2) == 0
print "Even numbers", np.extract(condition, a)
print "Non zero", np.nonzero(a)
```

Financial functions

NumPy has a number of financial functions, as follows:

◆ The `fv` function calculates the so-called future value. The future value gives the value of a financial instrument at a future date, based on certain assumptions.

◆ The `pv` function computes the present value. The present value is the value of an asset today.

◆ The `npv` function returns the net present value. The net present value is defined as the sum of all the present value cash flows.

◆ The `pmt` function computes the payment against loan principal plus interest.

◆ The `irr` function calculates the internal rate of return. The internal rate of return is the effective interested rate, which does not take into account inflation.

◆ The `mirr` function calculates the modified internal rate of return. The modified internal rate of return is an improved version of the internal rate of return.

◆ The `nper` function returns the number of periodic payments.

◆ The `rate` function calculates the rate of interest.

Time for action – determining future value

The future value gives the value of a financial instrument at a future date, based on certain assumptions. The future value depends on four parameters—the interest rate, the number of periods, a periodic payment, and the present value. In this tutorial, let's take an interest rate of three percent, quarterly payments of 10 for 5 years and present value of 1,000.

Call the `fv` function with the appropriate values to calculate the future value.

```
print "Future value", np.fv(0.03/4, 5 * 4, -10, -1000)
```

The future value is as follows:

```
Future value 1376.09633204
```

This corresponds with saving for 10 years, with quarterly additional savings of 10 at an interest rate of three percent. If we vary the number of years and if we save and keep the other parameters constant, we will get following plot:

What just happened?

We calculated the future value using the NumPy `fv` function starting with a present value of 1,000; interest rate of three percent; and quarterly payments of 10 for 5 years. We plotted the future value for various saving periods (see `futurevalue.py`).

```python
import numpy as np
from matplotlib.pyplot import plot, show

print "Future value", np.fv(0.03/4, 5 * 4, -10, -1000)

fvals = []

for i in xrange(1, 10):
    fvals.append(np.fv(.03/4, i * 4, -10, -1000))

plot(fvals, 'bo')
show()
```

Present value

The present value is the value of an asset today. The NumPy pv function can calculate the present value. This function mirrors the fv function and requires the interest rate, number of periods, and the periodic payment as well, but here we start with the future value.

Time for action – getting the present value

Let's reverse—compute the present value with numbers from the previous tutorial.

Plug in the figures from the *Time for action – determining future value* tutorial to calculate the present value.

```
print "Present value", np.pv(0.03/4, 5 * 4, -10, 1376.09633204)
```

This gives us 1,000 as expected apart from a tiny numerical error. Actually, it is not an error but a representation issue. We are dealing here with outgoing cash flow, that is the reason for the negative value.

```
Present value -999.999999999
```

What just happened?

We did the reverse computation of the previous *Time for action* tutorial to get the present value from the future value. This was done with the NumPy pv function.

Net present value

The net present value is defined as the sum of all the present value cash flows. The NumPy npv function returns the net present value of cash flows. The function requires two arguments, the rate and an array representing the cash flows.

Time for action – calculating the net present value

We will calculate the net present value for a randomly generated cash flow series. Perform the following steps to do so:

1. Generate five random values for the cash flow series. Insert -100 as the start value.

```
cashflows = np.random.randint(100, size=5)
cashflows = np.insert(cashflows, 0, -100)
print "Cashflows", cashflows
```

The cash flows would be shown as follows:

```
Cashflows [-100   38   48   90   17   36]
```

2. Call the `npv` function to calculate the net present value from the cash flow series we generated in the previous step. Use a rate of three percent.

```
print "Net present value", np.npv(0.03, cashflows)
```

The net present value would be shown as follows:

```
Net present value 107.435682443
```

What just happened?

We computed the net present value from a randomly generated cash flow series with the NumPy `npv` function (see `netpresentvalue.py`).

```
import numpy as np

cashflows = np.random.randint(100, size=5)
cashflows = np.insert(cashflows, 0, -100)
print "Cashflows", cashflows

print "Net present value", np.npv(0.03, cashflows)
```

Internal rate of return

The internal rate of return is the effective interest rate, which does not take into account inflation. The NumPy `irr` function returns the internal rate of return for a given cash flow series.

Time for action – determining the internal rate of return

Let's reuse the cash flow series from the *Time for action – calculating the net present value* tutorial.

Call the `irr` function with the cash flow series from the previous *Time for action* tutorial.

```
print "Internal rate of return", np.irr([-100, 38, 48, 90,
    17, 36])
```

The internal rate of return would be shown as follows:

```
Internal rate of return 0.373420226888
```

What just happened?

We calculated the internal rate of return from the cash flow series of the previous *Time for action* tutorial. The value was given by the NumPy `irr` function.

Periodic payments

The NumPy `pmt` function allows you to compute periodic payments for a loan based on an interest rate and the number of periodic payments.

Time for action – calculating the periodic payments

Suppose you have a loan of 1 million with interest rate of 10 percent. You have 30 years to pay the loan back. How much do you have to pay each month? Let's find out.

Call the `pmt` function with the values mentioned previously.

```
print "Payment", np.pmt(0.01/12, 12 * 30, 10000000)
```

The monthly payment would be shown as follows:

```
Payment -32163.9520447
```

What just happened?

We calculated the monthly payment for a loan of 1 million at an annual rate of 10 percent. Given that we have 30 years to repay the loan, the `pmt` function tells us that we need to pay 32,163.9520447 per month.

Number of payments

The NumPy `nper` function tells us how many periodic payments are necessary to pay off a loan. The required parameters are the interest rate of the loan, the fixed amount periodic payment, and the present value.

Time for action – determining the number of periodic payments

Consider a loan of 9,000 at a rate of 10 percent with fixed monthly payments of 100.

Find out how many payments are required with the NumPy `nper` function.

```
print "Number of payments", np.nper(0.10/12, -100, 9000)
```

The number of payments would be shown as follows:

```
Number of payments 167.047511801
```

What just happened?

We determined the number of payments needed to pay off a loan of 9,000 with an interest rate of 10 percent and monthly payments of 100. The number of payments returned was 167.

Interest rate

The NumPy `rate` function calculates the interest rate given the number of periodic payments, the payment amount or amounts, and the present value and future value.

Time for action – figuring out the rate

Let's take the values from the *Time for action – determining the number of periodic payments* tutorial and reverse compute the interest rate from the other parameters.

Fill in the numbers from the previous *Time for action* tutorial.

```
print "Interest rate", 12 * np.rate(167, -100, 9000, 0)
```

The interest rate is approximately 10 percent, as expected.

```
Interest rate 0.0999756420664
```

What just happened?

We used the NumPy `rate` function and the values from the previous *Time for action* tutorial to compute the interest rate of the loan. Ignoring the rounding errors we got the initial 10 percent we started with.

Window functions

Window functions are mathematical functions commonly used in signal processing. Applications include spectral analysis and filter design. These functions are defined to be 0 outside a specified domain. NumPy has a number of window functions such as `bartlett`, `blackman`, `hamming`, `hanning`, and `kaiser`. An example of the `hanning` function can be found in *Chapter 4, Convenience Functions for Your Convenience* and *Chapter 3, Get to Terms with Commonly Used Functions*.

Time for action – plotting the Bartlett window

The Bartlett window is a triangular smoothing window. Perform the following steps to plot the Bartlett window:

1. Call the NumPy `bartlett` function to calculate the Bartlett window.

   ```
   window = np.bartlett(42)
   ```

2. Plot the Bartlett window with Matplotlib, which is very easy.

   ```
   plot(window)
   show()
   ```

   The following is the Bartlett window, which is triangular, as expected:

What just happened?

We plotted the Bartlett window with the NumPy `bartlett` function.

Blackman window

The Blackman window is formed by summing the first three terms of cosines, as follows:

$$w(n) = 0.42 - 0.5\cos(2\pi n/M) + 0.08\cos(4\pi n/M)$$

The NumPy `blackman` function returns the Blackman window. The only parameter is the number of points in the output window. If this number is 0 or less than 0, an empty array is returned.

Time for action – smoothing stock prices with the Blackman window

Let's smooth the close prices from the small AAPL stock prices data file. Perform the following steps to do so:

1. Load the data into a NumPy array. Call the NumPy `blackman` function to form a window and then use this window to smooth the price signal.

```
closes=np.loadtxt('AAPL.csv', delimiter=',', usecols=(6,),
converters={1:datestr2num}, unpack=True)
N = int(sys.argv[1])
window = np.blackman(N)
smoothed = np.convolve(window/window.sum(),
   closes, mode='same')
```

2. Plot the smoothed prices with Matplotlib. We will omit the first five and the last five data points in this example. The reason for this is that there is a strong boundary effect.

```
plot(smoothed[N:-N], lw=2, label="smoothed")
plot(closes[N:-N], label="closes")
legend(loc='best')
show()
```

The closing prices of AAPL smoothed with the Blackman window should appear, as follows:

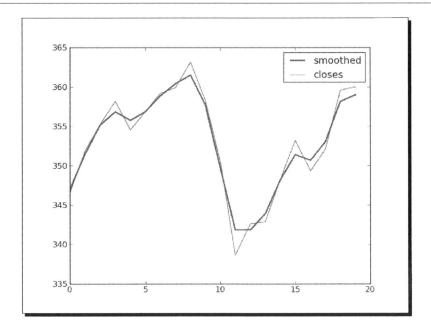

What just happened?

We plotted the closing price of AAPL from our sample data file that was smoothed using the Blackman window with the NumPy `blackman` function (see `plot_blackman.py`).

```
import numpy as np
from matplotlib.pyplot import plot, show, legend
from matplotlib.dates import datestr2num
import sys


closes=np.loadtxt('AAPL.csv', delimiter=',', usecols=(6,),
converters={1:datestr2num}, unpack=True)
N = int(sys.argv[1])
window = np.blackman(N)
smoothed = np.convolve(window/window.sum(), closes, mode='same')
plot(smoothed[N:-N], lw=2, label="smoothed")
plot(closes[N:-N], label="closes")
legend(loc='best')
show()
```

Hamming window

The Hamming window is formed by a weighted cosine. The formula is as follows:

$$w(n) = 0.54 + 0.46\cos\left(\frac{2\pi n}{M-1}\right) \qquad 0 \le n \le M-1$$

The NumPy `hamming` function returns the Hamming window. The only parameter is the number of points in the output window. If this number is 0 or less than 0, an empty array is returned.

Time for action – plotting the Hamming window

Let's plot the Hamming window. Perform the following steps to do so:

1. Call the NumPy `hamming` function to calculate the Hamming window.

   ```
   window = np.hamming(42)
   ```

2. Plot the window with Matplotlib.

   ```
   plot(window)
   show()
   ```

   The Hamming window plot is shown as follows:

What just happened?

We plotted the Hamming window with the NumPy `hamming` function.

Kaiser window

The Kaiser window is formed by the Bessel function. The formula is as follows:

$$w(n) = I_0\left(\beta\sqrt{1 - \frac{4n^2}{(M-1)^2}}\right)/I_0(\beta)$$

Here I0 is the zero order Bessel function The NumPy `kaiser` function returns the Kaiser window. The first parameter is the number of points in the output window. If this number is 0 or less than 0, an empty array is returned. The second parameter is the beta.

Time for action – plotting the Kaiser window

Let's plot the Kaiser window. Perform the following steps to do so:

1. Call the NumPy `kaiser` function to calculate the Kaiser window.

   ```
   window = np.kaiser(42, 14)
   ```

2. Plot the window with Matplotlib.

   ```
   plot(window)
   show()
   ```

   The Kaiser window would appear as follows:

What just happened?

We plotted the Hamming window with the NumPy `kaiser` function.

Special mathematical functions

We will end this chapter with some special mathematical functions. Bessel functions are solutions of the Bessel differential equations (visit http://en.wikipedia.org/wiki/Bessel_function). The modified Bessel function of the first kind 0th order is represented in NumPy by i0. The sinc function is represented in NumPy by a function with the same name and there is also a two-dimensional version of this function. sinc is a trigonometric function; for more details visit http://en.wikipedia.org/wiki/Sinc_function.

Time for action – plotting the modified Bessel function

Let's see what the modified Bessel function of the first kind 0th order looks like:

1. Compute evenly spaced values with the NumPy `linspace` function.

   ```
   x = np.linspace(0, 4, 100)
   ```

2. Call the NumPy i0 function to calculate the function values.

   ```
   vals = np.i0(x)
   ```

3. Plot the modified Bessel function with Matplotlib.

   ```
   plot(x, vals)
   show()
   ```

   The modified Bessel function would have the following output:

What just happened?

We plotted the modified Bessel function of the first kind 0th order with the NumPy i0 function.

sinc

The sinc function is widely used in Mathematics and signal processing. NumPy has a function with the same name. A two-dimensional function exists as well.

Time for action – plotting the sinc function

We will plot the sinc function. Perform the following steps to do so:

1. Compute evenly spaced values with the NumPy linspace function.

   ```
   x = np.linspace(0, 4, 100)
   ```

2. Call the NumPy sinc function to compute the function values.

   ```
   vals = np.sinc(x)
   ```

3. Plot the sinc function with Matplotlib.

   ```
   plot(x, vals)
   show()
   ```

   The sinc function would have the following output:

The `sinc2d` function requires a two-dimensional array. We can create it with the `outer` function resulting in the following plot:

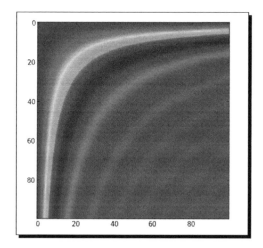

What just happened?

We plotted the well-known `sinc` function with the NumPy `sinc` function (see `plot_sinc.py`).

```
import numpy as np
from matplotlib.pyplot import plot, show

x = np.linspace(0, 4, 100)
vals = np.sinc(x)

plot(x, vals)
show()
```

We did the same for two dimensions (see `sinc2d.py`).

```
import numpy as np
from matplotlib.pyplot import imshow, show

x = np.linspace(0, 4, 100)
xx = np.outer(x, x)
vals = np.sinc(xx)

imshow(vals)
show()
```

Summary

This was a special chapter covering some of the more special NumPy topics. We covered sorting and searching, special functions, financial utilities, and window functions.

The next chapter will be about the very important subject of testing.

8
Assure Quality with Testing

Some programmers test only in production. If you are not one of them you're probably familiar with the concept of unit testing. Unit tests are automated tests written by a programmer to test his or her code. These tests could, for example, test a function or part of a function in isolation. Only a small unit of code is tested by each test. The benefits are increased confidence in the quality of the code, reproducible tests, and as a side effect, more clear code.

Python has good support for unit testing. Additionally, NumPy adds the `numpy.testing` *package to that for NumPy code unit testing.*

Test driven development (TDD) is one of the most important things that happened to software development. TDD focuses a lot on automated unit testing. The goal is to test automatically as much as possible of the code. The next time the code is changed we can run the tests and catch potential regressions. In other words functionality already present will still work.

This chapter's topics include:

- ◆ Unit testing
- ◆ Asserts
- ◆ Floating point precision

Assert functions

Unit tests usually use functions, which assert something as part of the test. When doing numerical calculations, often we have the fundamental issue of trying to compare floating-point numbers that are almost equal. For integers, comparison is a trivial operation, but for floating-point numbers it is not because of the inexact representation by computers. The numpy.testing package has a number of utility functions that test whether a precondition is true or not, taking into account the problem of floating-point comparisons:

Function	Description
assert_almost_equal	Raises an exception if two numbers are not equal up to a specified precision
assert_approx_equal	Raises an exception if two numbers are not equal up to a certain significance
assert_array_almost_equal	Raises an exception if two arrays are not equal up to a specified precision
assert_array_equal	Raises an exception if two arrays are not equal
assert_array_less	Raises an exception if two arrays do not have the same shape and the elements of the first array are strictly less than the elements of the second array
assert_equal	Raises an exception if two objects are not equal
assert_raises	Fails if a specified exception is not raised by a callable invoked with defined arguments
assert_warns	Fails if a specified warning is not thrown
assert_string_equal	Asserts that two strings are equal
assert_allclose	Raise an assertion if two objects are not equal up to desired tolerance

Time for action – asserting almost equal

Imagine that you have two numbers that are almost equal. Let's use the assert_almost_equal function to check whether they are equal:

1. Call the function with low precision (up to seven decimal places):

   ```
   print "Decimal 6", np.testing.assert_almost_equal(0.123456789,
   0.123456780, decimal=7)
   ```

   Note that no exception is raised, as you can see in the following result:

   ```
   Decimal 6 None
   ```

2. Call the function with higher precision (up to eight decimal places):

```
print "Decimal 7", np.testing.assert_almost_equal(0.123456789,
0.123456780, decimal=8)
```

The result is:

```
Decimal 7
Traceback (most recent call last):
   ...
raiseAssertionError(msg)
AssertionError:
Arrays are not almost equal
 ACTUAL: 0.123456789
 DESIRED: 0.12345678
```

What just happened?

We used the `assert_almost_equal` function from the NumPy `testing` package to check whether `0.123456789` and `0.123456780` are equal for different decimal precision.

Pop quiz – specifying decimal precision

Q1. Which parameter of the `assert_almost_equal` function specifies the decimal precision?

1. `decimal`
2. `precision`
3. `tolerance`
4. `significant`

Approximately equal arrays

The `assert_approx_equal` function raises an exception if two numbers are not equal up to a certain number of significant digits. The function result is an exception that is triggered by the condition:

```
abs(actual - expected) >= 10**-(significant - 1)
```

Time for action – asserting approximately equal

Let's take the numbers from the previous *Time for action* tutorial and let the
`assert_approx_equal` function work on them:

1. Call the function with low significance:

   ```
   print "Significance 8", np.testing.assert_approx_
   equal(0.123456789, 0.123456780,
   significant=8)
   ```

   The result is:

   ```
   Significance 8 None
   ```

2. Call the function with high significance:

   ```
   print "Significance 9",
   np.testing.assert_approx_equal
       (0.123456789, 0.123456780, significant=9)
   ```

   An exception is thrown:

   ```
   Significance 9
   Traceback (most recent call last):
     ...
   raiseAssertionError(msg)
   AssertionError:
   Items are not equal to 9 significant digits:
    ACTUAL: 0.123456789
    DESIRED: 0.12345678
   ```

What just happened?

We used the `assert_approx_equal` function from the `numpy.testing` package to
check whether `0.123456789` and `0.123456780` are equal for different decimal precision.

Almost equal arrays

The `assert_array_almost_equal` function raises an exception if two arrays are not
equal up to a specified precision. The function checks whether the two arrays have the
same shape. Then, the values of the arrays are compared element by element with:

```
|expected - actual| < 0.5 10-decimal
```

Time for action – asserting arrays almost equal

Let's form arrays with the values from the previous *Time for action* tutorial by adding a 0 to each array:

1. Calling the function with lower precision:

   ```
   print "Decimal 8", np.testing.assert_array_almost_equal([0,
      0.123456789], [0, 0.123456780], decimal=8)
   ```

   The result is:

   ```
   Decimal 8 None
   ```

2. Calling the function with higher precision:

   ```
   print "Decimal 9", np.testing.assert_array_almost_equal([0,
      0.123456789], [0, 0.123456780], decimal=9)
   ```

   An exception is thrown:

   ```
   Decimal 9
   Traceback (most recent call last):

      ...
   assert_array_compare
   raiseAssertionError(msg)
   AssertionError:
   Arrays are not almost equal


   (mismatch 50.0%)
   x: array([ 0.        ,  0.12345679])
    y: array([ 0.        ,  0.12345678])
   ```

What just happened?

We compared two arrays with the NumPy `array_almost_equal` function

Have a go hero – comparing array with different shapes

Use the NumPy `array_almost_equal` function to compare two arrays with different shapes.

Equal arrays

The `assert_array_equal` function raises an exception if two arrays are not equal. The shapes of the arrays have to be equal and the elements of each array must be equal. NaNs are allowed in the arrays. Alternatively, arrays can be compared with the `array_allclose` function. This function has the parameters `atol` (absolute tolerance) and `rtol` (relative tolerance). For two arrays a and b, these parameters satisfy the equation:

```
|a - b| <= (atol + rtol * |b|)
```

Time for action – comparing arrays

Let's compare two arrays with the functions we just mentioned. We will reuse the arrays from the previous *Time for action* tutorial and add a NaN to them:

1. Call the `array_allclose` function:

    ```
    print "Pass", np.testing.assert_allclose([0, 0.123456789,
    np.nan], [0, 0.123456780, np.nan], rtol=1e-7, atol=0)
    ```

    The result is:

    ```
    Pass None
    ```

2. Call the `array_equal` function:

    ```
    print "Fail", np.testing.assert_array_equal([0, 0.123456789,
    np.nan], [0, 0.123456780, np.nan])
    ```

    An exception is thrown:

    ```
    Fail
    Traceback (most recent call last):

      ...

    assert_array_compare
    raiseAssertionError(msg)
    AssertionError:
    Arrays are not equal


    (mismatch 50.0%)
    x: array([ 0.        ,  0.12345679,          nan])
     y: array([ 0.        ,   0.12345678,          nan])
    ```

What just happened?

We compared two arrays with the `array_allclose` function and the `array_equal` function.

Ordering arrays

The `assert_array_less` function raises an exception if two arrays do not have the same shape and the elements of the first array are strictly less than the elements of the second array.

Time for action – checking the array order

Let's check whether one array is strictly greater than another array:

1. Call the `assert_array_less` function with two strictly ordered arrays:

   ```
   print "Pass", np.testing.assert_array_less([0, 0.123456789,
   np.nan], [1, 0.23456780, np.nan])
   ```

   The result:

   ```
   Pass None
   ```

2. Call the `assert_array_less` function on failing the test:

   ```
   print "Fail", np.testing.assert_array_less([0, 0.123456789,

   np.nan], [0, 0.123456780, np.nan])
   ```

   An exception is thrown:

   ```
   Fail
   Traceback (most recent call last):
     ...
   raiseAssertionError(msg)
   AssertionError:
   Arrays are not less-ordered

   (mismatch 100.0%)
   x: array([ 0.        ,  0.12345679,          nan])
    y: array([ 0.        ,   0.12345678,          nan])
   ```

What just happened?

We checked the ordering of two arrays with the `assert_array_less` function.

Objects comparison

The `assert_equal` function raises an exception if two objects are not equal. The objects do not have to be NumPy arrays, they can also be lists, tuples, or dictionaries.

Time for action – comparing objects

Suppose you need to compare two tuples. We can use the `assert_equal` function to do that:

1. Call the `assert_equal` function:

```
print "Equal?", np.testing.assert_equal((1, 2), (1, 3))
```

An exception is thrown:

```
Equal?
Traceback (most recent call last):
  ...
raiseAssertionError(msg)
AssertionError:
Items are not equal:
item=1

 ACTUAL: 2
 DESIRED: 3
```

What just happened?

We compared two tuples with the `assert_equal` function—an exception was raised because the tuples were not equal to each other.

String comparison

The `assert_string_equal` function asserts that two strings are equal. If the test fails an exception is thrown and the difference between the strings is shown. The case of the string characters matters.

Time for action – comparing strings

Let's compare strings. Both strings are the word `"NumPy"`:

1. Call the `assert_string_equal` function to compare a string with itself. This test, of course, should pass:

   ```
   print "Pass", np.testing.assert_string_equal("NumPy", "NumPy")
   ```

   The test passes:

   ```
   Pass None
   ```

2. Call the `assert_string_equal` function to compare a string with another string with the same letters but different casing. This test should throw an exception:

   ```
   print "Fail", np.testing.assert_string_equal("NumPy", "Numpy")
   ```

   An exception is thrown:

   ```
   Fail
   Traceback (most recent call last):

      ...
   raiseAssertionError(msg)
   AssertionError: Differences in strings:
   - NumPy?       ^
   + Numpy?       ^
   ```

What just happened?

We compared two strings with the `assert_string_equal` function. The test threw an exception when the casing did not match.

Floating point comparisons

The representation of floating-point numbers in computers is not exact. This leads to issues when comparing floating-point numbers. The `assert_array_almost_equal_nulp` and `assert_array_max_ulp` NumPy functions provide consistent floating-point comparisons. **ULP** stands for **Unit of Least Precision** of floating point numbers. According to the IEEE 754 specification, a half ULP precision is required for elementary arithmetic operations. You can compare this to a ruler. A metric system ruler usually has ticks for millimetres, but beyond that you can only estimate half millimetres.

Machine epsilon is the largest relative rounding error in floating point arithmetic. Machine epsilon is equal to ULP relative to one. The NumPy `finfo` function allows us to determine the machine epsilon. The Python standard library also can give you the machine epsilon value. The value should be the same as that given by NumPy.

Time for action – comparing with assert_array_almost_equal_nulp

Let's see the `assert_array_almost_equal_nulp` function in action:

1. Determine the machine epsilon with the `finfo` function:

```
eps = np.finfo(float).eps
print "EPS", eps
```

The epsilon would be:

```
EPS 2.22044604925e-16
```

2. Compare two almost equal floats: Compare `1.0` with `1 + `epsilon (`eps`) using the `assert_almost_equal_nulp` function. Do the same for `1 + 2 * `epsilon (`eps`):

```
print "1",
np.testing.assert_array_almost_equal_nulp(1.0, 1.0 + eps)
print "2",
np.testing.assert_array_almost_equal_nulp(1.0, 1.0 + 2 * eps)
```

The result:

```
1 None
2
Traceback (most recent call last):
  ...
assert_array_almost_equal_nulp
raiseAssertionError(msg)
AssertionError: X and Y are not equal to 1 ULP (max is 2)
```

What just happened?

We determined the machine epsilon with the `finfo` function. We then compared `1.0` with `1 + `epsilon (`eps`) with the `assert_almost_equal_nulp` function. This test passed, however, adding another epsilon resulted in an exception.

Comparison of floats with more ULPs

The `assert_array_max_ulp` function allows you to specify an upper bound for the number of ULPs you would allow. The `maxulp` parameter accepts an integer value for the limit. The value of this parameter is 1 by default.

Time for action – comparing using maxulp of 2

Let's do the same comparisons as in the previous *Time for action* tutorial, but specify a `maxulp` of 2 when necessary:

1. Determine the machine epsilon with the `finfo` function:

    ```
    eps = np.finfo(float).eps
    print "EPS", eps
    ```

    The epsilon would be:

    ```
    EPS 2.22044604925e-16
    ```

2. Do the comparisons as done in the previous *Time for action* tutorial, but use the `assert_array_max_ulp` function with the appropriate `maxulp` value:

    ```
    print "1", np.testing.assert_array_max_ulp(1.0, 1.0 + eps)
    print "2", np.testing.assert_array_max_ulp(1.0, 1 + 2 * eps,
    maxulp=2)
    ```

    The output:

    ```
    1 1.0
    2 2.0
    ```

What just happened?

We compared the same values as the previous *Time for action* tutorial, but specified a `maxulp` of 2 in the second comparison. Using the `assert_array_max_ulp` function with the appropriate `maxulp` value, these tests passed with a return value of the number of ULPs.

Unit tests

Unit tests are automated tests, which test a small piece of code, usually a function or method. Python has the PyUnit API for unit testing. As NumPy users we can make use of the assert functions we saw in action before.

Time for action – writing a unit test

We will write tests for a simple factorial function. The tests will check for the so called happy path and for abnormal conditions.

1. We start by writing the factorial function

```
def factorial(n):
  if n == 0:
    return 1

  if n < 0:
    raise ValueError, "Unexpected negative value"

  return np.arange(1, n+1).cumprod()
```

The code is using the `arange` and `cumprod` functions we have already seen to create arrays and calculate the cumulative product, but we added a few checks for boundary conditions.

2. Now we will write the unit test. Let's write a class that will contain the unit tests. It extends the `TestCase` class from the `unittest` module which is part of standard Python. We test for calling the factorial function with:

   ❏ a positive number, the happy path
   ❏ boundary condition 0
   ❏ negative numbers, which should result in an error

```
class FactorialTest(unittest.TestCase):
  def test_factorial(self):
    #Test for the factorial of 3 that should pass.
    self.assertEqual(6, factorial(3)[-1])
    np.testing.assert_equal(np.array([1, 2, 6]), factorial(3))

  def test_zero(self):
    #Test for the factorial of 0 that should pass.
    self.assertEqual(1, factorial(0))

  def test_negative(self):
    #Test for the factorial of negative numbers that should fail.
    # It should throw a ValueError, but we expect IndexError
    self.assertRaises(IndexError, factorial(-10))
```

We rigged one of the tests to fail as you can see in the following output:

```
$ python unit_test.py
.E.
=================================================================
====
ERROR: test_negative (__main__.FactorialTest)
-----------------------------------------------------------------
----
Traceback (most recent call last):
  File "unit_test.py", line 26, in test_negative
self.assertRaises(IndexError, factorial(-10))
  File "unit_test.py", line 9, in factorial
raiseValueError, "Unexpected negative value"
ValueError: Unexpected negative value


-----------------------------------------------------------------
----
Ran 3 tests in 0.003s


FAILED (errors=1)
```

What just happened?

We made some happy path tests for factorial function code. We let the boundary condition test fail on purpose (see unit_test.py):

```
import numpy as np
import unittest


def factorial(n):
  if n == 0:
    return 1

  if n < 0:
    raise ValueError, "Unexpected negative value"

  return np.arange(1, n+1).cumprod()


class FactorialTest(unittest.TestCase):
  def test_factorial(self):
```

```
        #Test for the factorial of 3 that should pass.
        self.assertEqual(6, factorial(3)[-1])
        np.testing.assert_equal(np.array([1, 2, 6]), factorial(3))

    def test_zero(self):
        #Test for the factorial of 0 that should pass.
        self.assertEqual(1, factorial(0))

    def test_negative(self):
        #Test for the factorial of negative numbers that should fail.
        # It should throw a ValueError, but we expect IndexError
        self.assertRaises(IndexError, factorial(-10))


if __name__ == '__main__':
    unittest.main()
```

Nose tests decorators

A nose is an organ above the mouth that is used by humans and animals to breathe and smell. It is also a Python framework that makes (unit) testing easier. Nose helps you organize tests. According to the nose documentation: "any python source file, directory, or package that matches the testMatch regular expression (by default: `(?:^|[b_.-])[Tt]est)` will be collected as a test". Nose makes extensive use of decorators. Python decorators are annotations that indicate something about a method or a function. The numpy.testing module has a number of decorators:

Decorator	Description
numpy.testing.decorators.deprecated	Filters deprecation warnings when running tests.
numpy.testing.decorators.knownfailureif	Raises KnownFailureTest exception based on a condition.
numpy.testing.decorators.setastest	Marks a function as being a test or not being a test.
numpy.testing.decorators.skipif	Raises SkipTest exception based on a condition.
numpy.testing.decorators.slow	Labels test functions or methods as slow.

Additionally we can call the decorate_methods function to apply decorators on methods of a class matching a regular expression or a string.

Time for action – decorating tests

We will apply the `setastest` decorator directly to test functions. Then we will apply the same decorator to a method to disable it. Also we will skip one of the tests and fail another. First we will install `nose` in case you don't have it yet.

1. Install `nose` with `setuptools`

    ```
    easy_install nose
    ```

    Or `pip`:

    ```
    pip install nose
    ```

2. We will apply one function as being a test and another as not being a test.

    ```
    @setastest(False)
    def test_false():
       pass

    @setastest(True)
    def test_true():
       pass
    ```

3. We can skip tests with the `skipif` decorator. Let's use a condition that always leads to a test being skipped.

    ```
    @skipif(True)
    def test_skip():
       pass
    ```

4. Add a test function that always passes. Then decorate it with the `knownfailureif` decorator so that the test always fails.

    ```
    @knownfailureif(True)
    def test_alwaysfail():
        pass
    ```

5. We will define some test classes with methods that normally should be executed by `nose`.

    ```
    class TestClass():
      def test_true2(self):
        pass

    class TestClass2():
      def test_false2(self):
        pass
    ```

6. Let's disable the second test method from the previous step.

```
decorate_methods(TestClass2, setastest(False), 'test_false2')
```

7. We can run the tests with the following command:

```
nosetests -v decorator_setastest.py

decorator_setastest.TestClass.test_true2 ... ok

decorator_setastest.test_true ... ok

decorator_test.test_skip ... SKIP: Skipping test: test_skipTest
skipped due to test condition

decorator_test.test_alwaysfail ... ERROR


=================================================================
====

ERROR: decorator_test.test_alwaysfail

-----------------------------------------------------------------
----

Traceback (most recent call last):
  File ".../nose/case.py", line 197, in runTest
self.test(*self.arg)
  File .../numpy/testing/decorators.py", line 213, in knownfailer
raiseKnownFailureTest(msg)
KnownFailureTest: Test skipped due to known failure


-----------------------------------------------------------------
----

Ran 4 tests in 0.001s


FAILED (SKIP=1, errors=1)
```

What just happened?

We decorated some functions and methods as not being tests, so that they were ignored by nose. We skipped one test and failed another too. We did this by applying decorators directly and with the decorate_methods function (see decorator_test.py):

```
from numpy.testing.decorators import setastest
from numpy.testing.decorators import skipif
from numpy.testing.decorators import knownfailureif
from numpy.testing import decorate_methods
```

```
@setastest(False)
def test_false():
  pass

@setastest(True)
def test_true():
  pass

@skipif(True)
def test_skip():
    pass

@knownfailureif(True)
def test_alwaysfail():
    pass


class TestClass():
  def test_true2(self):
    pass


class TestClass2():
  def test_false2(self):
    pass

decorate_methods(TestClass2, setastest(False), 'test_false2')
```

Docstrings

Docstrings are strings embedded in Python code that resemble interactive sessions.
These strings can be used to test certain assumptions, or just provide examples.
The `numpy.testing` module has a function to run these tests.

Time for action – executing doctests

Let's write a simple example that is supposed to calculate the well-known factorial, but doesn't cover all the possible boundary conditions. In other words some tests will fail.

1. The docstring will look like text you would see in a Python shell (including a prompt). We will rig one of the tests to fail, just to see what will happen.

```
"""
Test for the factorial of 3 that should pass.
>>> factorial(3)
6

Test for the factorial of 0 that should fail.
>>> factorial(0)
1
"""
```

2. We will write the following line of NumPy code to compute the factorial:

```
return np.arange(1, n+1).cumprod()[-1]
```

We want this code to fail from time to time for demonstration purposes.

3. We can run the `doctest` by calling the `rundocs` function of the `numpy.testing` module for instance in the Python shell.

```
>>>from numpy.testing import rundocs
>>>rundocs('docstringtest.py')
Traceback (most recent call last):
  File "<stdin>", line 1, in <module>
  File ".../numpy/testing/utils.py", line 998, in rundocs
raiseAssertionError("Some doctests failed:\n%s" % "\n".join(msg))
AssertionError: Some doctests failed:
*********************************************************************
****
File "docstringtest.py", line 10, in docstringtest.factorial
Failed example:
factorial(0)
Exception raised:
Traceback (most recent call last):
    File ".../doctest.py", line 1254, in __run
compileflags, 1) in test.globs
```

```
        File "<doctestdocstringtest.factorial[1]>", line 1, in
    <module>
    factorial(0)
        File "docstringtest.py", line 13, in factorial
    return np.arange(1, n+1).cumprod()[-1]
    IndexError: index -1 is out of bounds for axis 0 with size 0
```

What just happened?

We wrote a docstring test which didn't take into account 0 and negative numbers. We run the test with the `rundocs` function from the `numpy.testing` module and got an index error as a result (see `docstringtest.py`):

```
import numpy as np


def factorial(n):
    """
    Test for the factorial of 3 that should pass.
    >>> factorial(3)
    6

    Test for the factorial of 0 that should fail.
    >>> factorial(0)
    1
    """
    return np.arange(1, n+1).cumprod()[-1]
```

Summary

We learned about testing and NumPy testing utilities in this chapter. We covered unit testing, docstring tests, assert functions, and floating point precision. Most of the NumPy assert functions take care of the complexities of floating point numbers. We demonstrated NumPy decorators that can be used by `nose`. Decorators make testing easier and document the developer intention.

The topic of the next chapter is Matplotlib—the Python scientific visualization and graphing open-source library.

9
Plotting with Matplotlib

Matplotlib is a very useful Python plotting library. It integrates nicely with NumPy but is a separate open source project. You can find a gallery of beautiful examples at `http://matplotlib.sourceforge.net/gallery.html`.

Matplotlib also has utility functions to download and manipulate data from Yahoo Finance. We will see several examples of stock charts.

This chapter features extended coverage of:

- ◆ Simple plots
- ◆ Subplots
- ◆ Histograms
- ◆ Plot customization
- ◆ Three-dimensional plots
- ◆ Contour plots
- ◆ Animation
- ◆ Logplots

Simple plots

The `matplotlib.pyplot` package contains functionality for simple plots. It is important to remember that each subsequent function call changes the state of the current plot. Eventually we will want to either save the plot in a file or display it with the `show` function. However, if we are in IPython running on a Qt or Wx backend the figure will be updated interactively without waiting for the `show` function. This is comparable to the way text output is printed on the fly.

Time for action – plotting a polynomial function

To illustrate how plotting works, let's display some polynomial graphs. We will use the NumPy polynomial function `poly1d` to create a polynomial.

1. Take the standard input values as polynomial coefficients. Use the NumPy `poly1d` function to create a polynomial.

   ```
   func = np.poly1d(np.array([1, 2, 3, 4]).astype(float))
   ```

2. Create the x values with the NumPy `linspace` function. Use the range -10 to 10 and create 30 even spaced values.

   ```
   x = np.linspace(-10, 10, 30)
   ```

3. Calculate the polynomial values using the polynomial that we created in the first step.

   ```
   y = func(x)
   ```

4. Call the `plot` function; this does not immediately display the graph.

   ```
   plt.plot(x, y)
   ```

5. Add a label to the x axis with `xlabel` function.

   ```
   plt.xlabel('x')
   ```

6. Add a label to the y axis with `ylabel` function.

   ```
   plt.ylabel('y(x)')
   ```

7. Call the `show` function to display the graph.

   ```
   plt.show()
   ```

Here is a plot with polynomial coefficients 1, 2, 3, and 4:

What just happened?

We displayed a graph of a polynomial on our screen. We added labels to the x and y axis (see polyplot.py):

```
import numpy as np
import matplotlib.pyplot as plt

func = np.poly1d(np.array([1, 2, 3, 4]).astype(float))
x = np.linspace(-10, 10, 30)
y = func(x)

plt.plot(x, y)
plt.xlabel('x')
plt.ylabel('y(x)')
plt.show()
```

Pop quiz – the plot function

Q1. What does the plot function do?

1. It displays two-dimensional plots on screen.

2. It saves an image of a two-dimensional plot in a file.

3. It does both 1 and 2.

4. It does neither 1, 2, or 3.

Plot format string

The `plot` function accepts an unlimited number of arguments. In the previous section we gave it two arrays as arguments. We could also specify the line color and style with an optional format string. By default, it is a solid blue line denoted as `b-`, but you can specify a different color and style such as red dashes.

Time for action – plotting a polynomial and its derivative

Let's plot a polynomial and its first order derivative using the `derive` function with `m` as `1`. We already did the first part in the previous *Time for action* tutorial. We want to have two different line styles to be able to discern what is what.

1. Create and differentiate the polynomial.

```
func = np.poly1d(np.array([1, 2, 3, 4]).astype(float))
func1 = func.deriv(m=1)
x = np.linspace(-10, 10, 30)
y = func(x)
y1 = func1(x)
```

2. Plot the polynomial and its derivative in two different styles: red circles and green dashes. You cannot see the colors in a print copy of this book so you will have to try it out for yourself.

```
plt.plot(x, y, 'ro', x, y1, 'g--')
plt.xlabel('x')
plt.ylabel('y')
plt.show()
```

The graph again with polynomial coefficients 1, 2, 3, and 4:

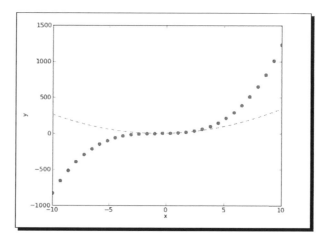

What just happened?

We plotted a polynomial and its derivative using two different line styles and one call of the plot function (see `polyplot2.py`):

```
import numpy as np
import matplotlib.pyplot as plt

func = np.poly1d(np.array([1, 2, 3, 4]).astype(float))
func1 = func.deriv(m=1)
x = np.linspace(-10, 10, 30)
y = func(x)
y1 = func1(x)

plt.plot(x, y, 'ro', x, y1, 'g--')
plt.xlabel('x')
plt.ylabel('y')
plt.show()
```

Subplots

At a certain point you will have too many lines in one plot. Still, you would like to have everything grouped together. We can achieve this with the `subplot` function.

Time for action – plotting a polynomial and its derivatives

Let's plot a polynomial and its first and second derivative. We will make three subplots for the sake of clarity:

1. Create a polynomial and its derivatives using the following code.

    ```
    func = np.poly1d(np.array([1, 2, 3, 4]).astype(float))
    x = np.linspace(-10, 10, 30)
    y = func(x)
    func1 = func.deriv(m=1)
    y1 = func1(x)
    func2 = func.deriv(m=2)
    y2 = func2(x)
    ```

2. Create the first subplot of the polynomial with the `subplot` function. The first parameter of this function is the number of rows, the second parameter is the number of columns, and the third parameter is an index number starting with 1. Alternatively, you can combine the three parameters into a single number such as `311`. The subplots will be organized in 3 rows and 1 column. Give the subplot the title `"Polynomial"`. Make a solid red line.

```
plt.subplot(311)
plt.plot(x, y, 'r-')
plt.title("Polynomial")
```

3. Create the third subplot of the first derivative with the `subplot` function. Give the subplot the title `"First Derivative"`. Use a line of blue triangles.

```
plt.subplot(312)
plt.plot(x, y1, 'b^')
plt.title("First Derivative")
```

4. Create the second subplot of the second derivative with the `subplot` function. Give the subplot the title `"Second Derivative"`. Use a line of green circles.

```
plt.subplot(313)
plt.plot(x, y2, 'go')
plt.title("Second Derivative")
plt.xlabel('x')
plt.ylabel('y')
plt.show()
```

The three subplots with polynomial coefficients 1, 2, 3, and 4:

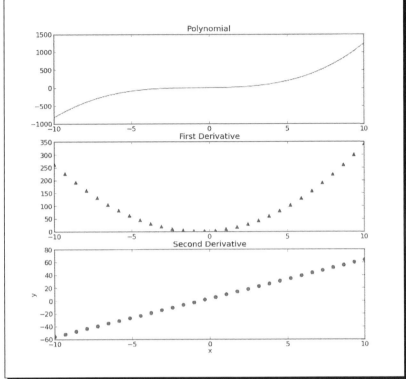

What just happened?

We plotted a polynomial and its first and second derivative using three different line styles and three subplots in 3 rows and 1 column (see `polyplot3.py`):

```
import numpy as np
import matplotlib.pyplot as plt

func = np.poly1d(np.array([1, 2, 3, 4]).astype(float))
x = np.linspace(-10, 10, 30)
y = func(x)
func1 = func.deriv(m=1)
y1 = func1(x)
func2 = func.deriv(m=2)
y2 = func2(x)

plt.subplot(311)
plt.plot(x, y, 'r-')
```

```
plt.title("Polynomial")
plt.subplot(312)
plt.plot(x, y1, 'b^')
plt.title("First Derivative")
plt.subplot(313)
plt.plot(x, y2, 'go')
plt.title("Second Derivative")
plt.xlabel('x')
plt.ylabel('y')
plt.show()
```

Finance

Matplotlib can help us monitor our stock investments. The `matplotlib.finance` package has utilities with which we can download stock quotes from Yahoo Finance (`http://finance.yahoo.com/`). The data can then be plotted as candlesticks.

Time for action – plotting a year's worth of stock quotes

We can plot a year's worth of stock quotes data with the `matplotlib.finance` package. This will require a connection to Yahoo Finance, which will be the data source.

1. Determine the start date by subtracting 1 year from today.

```
from matplotlib.dates import DateFormatter
from matplotlib.dates import DayLocator
from matplotlib.dates import MonthLocator
from matplotlib.finance import quotes_historical_yahoo
from matplotlib.finance import candlestick
import sys
from datetime import date
import matplotlib.pyplot as plt
today = date.today()
start = (today.year - 1, today.month, today.day)
```

2. We need to create so-called locators. These objects from the `matplotlib.dates` package are needed to locate months and days on the x-axis.

```
alldays = DayLocator()
months = MonthLocator()
```

3. Create a date formatter to format the dates on the x axis. This formatter will create a string containing the short name of a month and the year.

```
month_formatter = DateFormatter("%b %Y")
```

4. Download the stock quote data from Yahoo finance with the following code:

```
quotes = quotes_historical_yahoo(symbol, start, today)
```

5. Create a Matplotlib `figure` object—this is a top-level container for plot components.

```
fig = plt.figure()
```

6. Add a subplot to the figure.

```
ax = fig.add_subplot(111)
```

7. Set the major locator on the x axis to the months locator. This locator is responsible for the big ticks on the x axis.

```
ax.xaxis.set_major_locator(months)
```

8. Set the minor locator on the x axis to the days locator. This locator is responsible for the small ticks on the x axis.

```
ax.xaxis.set_minor_locator(alldays)
```

9. Set the major formatter on the x axis to the months formatter. This formatter is responsible for the labels of the big ticks on the x axis.

```
ax.xaxis.set_major_formatter(month_formatter)
```

10. A function in the `matplotlib.finance` package allows us to display candlesticks. Create the candlesticks using the quotes data. It is possible to specify the width of the candlesticks. For now, use the default value.

```
candlestick(ax, quotes)
```

11. Format the labels on the x axis as dates. This should rotate the labels on the x axis, so that they fit better.

```
fig.autofmt_xdate()
plt.show()
```

The candlestick chart for **DISH (Dish Network Corp.)** would appear as follows:

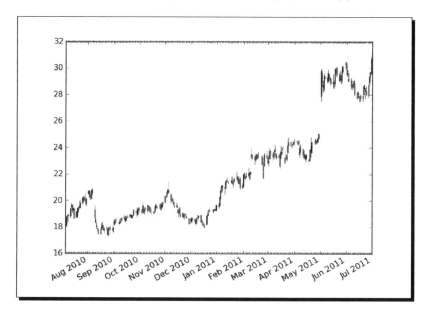

What just happened?

We downloaded a year's worth of data from Yahoo Finance. We charted this data using candlesticks (see `candlesticks.py`):

```
from matplotlib.dates import DateFormatter
from matplotlib.dates import DayLocator
from matplotlib.dates import MonthLocator
from matplotlib.finance import quotes_historical_yahoo
from matplotlib.finance import candlestick
import sys
from datetime import date
import matplotlib.pyplot as plt

today = date.today()
start = (today.year - 1, today.month, today.day)

alldays = DayLocator()
months = MonthLocator()
month_formatter = DateFormatter("%b %Y")

symbol = 'DISH'

if len(sys.argv) == 2:
```

```
    symbol = sys.argv[1]

quotes = quotes_historical_yahoo(symbol, start, today)

fig = plt.figure()
ax = fig.add_subplot(111)
ax.xaxis.set_major_locator(months)
ax.xaxis.set_minor_locator(alldays)
ax.xaxis.set_major_formatter(month_formatter)

candlestick(ax, quotes)
fig.autofmt_xdate()
plt.show()
```

Histograms

Histograms visualize the distribution of numerical data. Matplotlib has the handy `hist` function that graphs histograms. The `hist` function has two arguments—the array containing the data and the number of bars.

Time for action – charting stock price distributions

Let's chart the stock price distribution of quotes from Yahoo Finance.

1. Download the data going back 1 year.

   ```
   today = date.today()
   start = (today.year - 1, today.month, today.day)

   quotes = quotes_historical_yahoo(symbol, start, today)
   ```

2. The quotes data in the previous step is stored in a Python list. Convert this to a NumPy array and extract the close prices.

   ```
   quotes = np.array(quotes)
   close = quotes.T[4]
   ```

3. Draw the histogram with a reasonable number of bars.

   ```
   plt.hist(close, np.sqrt(len(close)))
   plt.show()
   ```

The histogram for DISH would appear as follows:

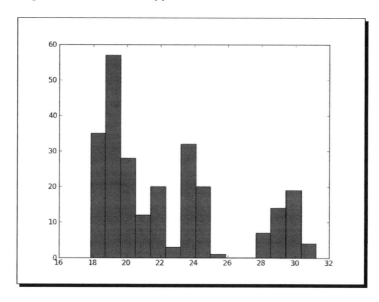

What just happened?

We charted the stock price distribution of DISH as histogram (see `stockhistogram.py`):

```
from matplotlib.finance import quotes_historical_yahoo
import sys
from datetime import date
import matplotlib.pyplot as plt
import numpy as np

today = date.today()
start = (today.year - 1, today.month, today.day)

symbol = 'DISH'

if len(sys.argv) == 2:
    symbol = sys.argv[1]

quotes = quotes_historical_yahoo(symbol, start, today)
quotes = np.array(quotes)
close = quotes.T[4]

plt.hist(close, np.sqrt(len(close)))
plt.show()
```

Have a go hero – drawing a bell curve

Overlay a bell curve (related to Gaussian or normal distribution) using the average price and standard deviation. This is, of course, only an exercise.

Logarithmic plots

Logarithmic plots are useful when the data has a wide range of values. Matplotlib has the functions `semilogx` (logarithmic x axis), `semilogy` (logarithmic y axis), and `loglog` (x and y axis logarithmic).

Time for action – plotting stock volume

Stock volume varies a lot, so let's plot it on a logarithmic scale. First we need to download historical data from Yahoo Finance, extract the dates and volume, create locators and a date formatter, create the figure, and add to it a subplot. We already went through these steps in the previous *Time for action* tutorial, so we will skip them here.

1. Plot the volume using a logarithmic scale.

   ```
   plt.semilogy(dates, volume)
   ```

   Now set the locators and format the x-axis as dates. Instructions for these steps can be found in the previous *Time for action* tutorial as well. The stock volume using a logarithmic scale for DISH would appear as follows:

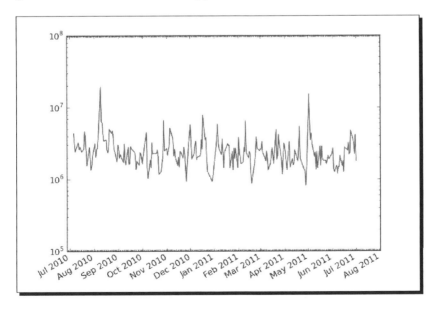

What just happened?

We plotted stock volume using a logarithmic scale (see `logy.py`):

```
from matplotlib.finance import quotes_historical_yahoo
from matplotlib.dates import DateFormatter
from matplotlib.dates import DayLocator
from matplotlib.dates import MonthLocator
import sys
from datetime import date
import matplotlib.pyplot as plt
import numpy as np

today = date.today()
start = (today.year - 1, today.month, today.day)

symbol = 'DISH'

if len(sys.argv) == 2:
    symbol = sys.argv[1]

quotes = quotes_historical_yahoo(symbol, start, today)
quotes = np.array(quotes)
dates = quotes.T[0]
volume = quotes.T[5]


alldays = DayLocator()
months = MonthLocator()
month_formatter = DateFormatter("%b %Y")

fig = plt.figure()
ax = fig.add_subplot(111)
plt.semilogy(dates, volume)
ax.xaxis.set_major_locator(months)
ax.xaxis.set_minor_locator(alldays)
ax.xaxis.set_major_formatter(month_formatter)
fig.autofmt_xdate()
plt.show
```

Scatter plots

A scatter plot displays values for two numerical variables in the same data set. The Matplotlib `scatter` function creates a scatter plot. Optionally, we can specify the color and size of the data points in the plot as well as alpha transparency.

Time for action – plotting price and volume returns with scatter plot

We can easily make a scatter plot of the stock price and volume returns. Again, let's download the necessary data from Yahoo Finance.

1. The `quotes` data in the previous step is stored in a Python list. Convert this to a NumPy array and extract the close and volume values.

```
dates = quotes.T[4]
volume = quotes.T[5]
```

2. Calculate the close price and volume returns.

```
ret = np.diff(close)/close[:-1]
volchange = np.diff(volume)/volume[:-1]
```

3. Create a Matplotlib `figure` object

```
fig = pyplot.figure()
```

4. Add a `subplot` to the figure.

```
ax = fig.add_subplot(111)
```

5. Create the `scatter` plot with the color of the data points linked to the close return, and the size linked to the volume change.

```
ax.scatter(ret, volchange, c=ret * 100,
    s=volchange * 100, alpha=0.5
```

6. Set the `title` of the plot and put a `grid` on it.

```
ax.set_title('Close and volume returns')
ax.grid(True)

pyplot.show()
```

The scatter plot for DISH will appear as follows:

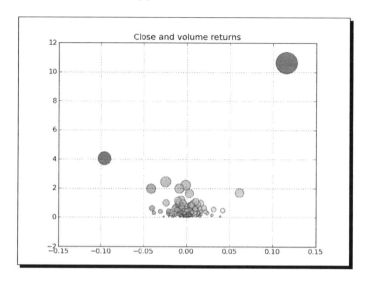

What just happened?

We made a scatter plot of the close price and volume returns for DISH (see `scatterprice.py`):

```
from matplotlib.finance import quotes_historical_yahoo
import sys
from datetime import date
import matplotlib.pyplot as plt
import numpy as np

today = date.today()
start = (today.year - 1, today.month, today.day)

symbol = 'DISH'

if len(sys.argv) == 2:
   symbol = sys.argv[1]

quotes = quotes_historical_yahoo(symbol, start, today)
quotes = np.array(quotes)
close = quotes.T[4]
volume = quotes.T[5]
ret = np.diff(close)/close[:-1]
volchange = np.diff(volume)/volume[:-1]
```

```
fig = plt.figure()
ax = fig.add_subplot(111)
ax.scatter(ret, volchange, c=ret * 100, s=volchange * 100, alpha=0.5)
ax.set_title('Close and volume returns')
ax.grid(True)

plt.show()
```

Fill between

The `fill_between` function fills a region of a plot with a specified color. We can also choose an alpha channel value. The function also has a `where` parameter so that we can shade a region based on a condition.

Time for action – shading plot regions based on a condition

Imagine that you want to shade the region of a stock chart, where the closing price is below average, with a different color than when it is above the mean. The `fill_between` function is the best choice for the job. We will again omit the steps of downloading historical data going back 1 year, extracting dates and close prices, and creating locators and date formatter.

1. Create a Matplotlib figure object.

```
fig = plt.figure()
```

2. Add a subplot to the figure.

```
ax = fig.add_subplot(111)
```

3. Plot the closing price.

```
ax.plot(dates, close)
```

4. Shade the regions of the plot below the closing price using different colors depending whether the values are below or above the average price.

```
plt.fill_between(dates, close.min(), close,
   where=close>close.mean(), facecolor="green", alpha=0.4)
plt.fill_between(dates, close.min(), close,
   where=close<close.mean(), facecolor="red", alpha=0.4)
```

Now we can finish the plot by setting locators and formatting the x-axis values as dates. The stock price using conditional shading for DISH:

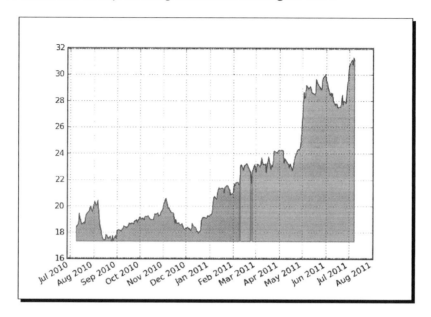

What just happened?

We shaded the region of a stock chart, where the closing price is below average, with a different color than when it is above the mean (see `fillbetween.py`):

```
from matplotlib.finance import quotes_historical_yahoo
from matplotlib.dates import DateFormatter
from matplotlib.dates import DayLocator
from matplotlib.dates import MonthLocator
import sys
from datetime import date
import matplotlib.pyplot as plt
import numpy as np


today = date.today()
start = (today.year - 1, today.month, today.day)


symbol = 'DISH'


if len(sys.argv) == 2:
    symbol = sys.argv[1]


quotes = quotes_historical_yahoo(symbol, start, today)
```

```
quotes = np.array(quotes)
dates = quotes.T[0]
close = quotes.T[4]


alldays = DayLocator()
months = MonthLocator()
month_formatter = DateFormatter("%b %Y")

fig = plt.figure()
ax = fig.add_subplot(111)
ax.plot(dates, close)
plt.fill_between(dates, close.min(), close, where=close>close.mean(),
facecolor="green", alpha=0.4)
plt.fill_between(dates, close.min(), close, where=close<close.mean(),
facecolor="red", alpha=0.4)
ax.xaxis.set_major_locator(months)
ax.xaxis.set_minor_locator(alldays)
ax.xaxis.set_major_formatter(month_formatter)
ax.grid(True)
fig.autofmt_xdate()
plt.show()
```

Legend and annotations

Legends and annotations are essential for good plots. We can create transparent legends with the `legend` function and let Matplotlib figure out where to place them. Also, with the `annotate` function we can put annotations very accurately on a plot. There are a large number of annotation and arrow styles.

Time for action – using legend and annotations

In *Chapter 3, Getting to Terms with Commonly Used Functions* we learned how to calculate the exponential moving average of stock prices. We will plot the close price of a stock and three of its exponential moving averages. To clarify the plot, we will add a legend. Also, we will indicate crossovers of two of the averages with annotations. Some steps are again omitted to avoid repetition.

1. **Calculate and plot the exponential moving averages**: Go back to *Chapter 3, Getting to Terms with Commonly Used Functions* if needed and review the exponential moving average algorithm. Calculate and plot the exponential moving averages of 9, 12, and 15 periods.

```
emas = []
for i in range(9, 18, 3):
    weights = np.exp(np.linspace(-1., 0., i))
    weights /= weights.sum()
    ema = np.convolve(weights, close)[i-1:-i+1]
    idx = (i - 6)/3
    ax.plot(dates[i-1:], ema, lw=idx, label="EMA(%s)" % (i))
    data = np.column_stack((dates[i-1:], ema))
    emas.append(np.rec.fromrecords(
        data, names=["dates", "ema"]))
```

Notice that the `plot` function call needs a label for the legend. We stored the moving averages in record arrays for the next step.

2. Let's find the crossover points of the first two moving averages

```
first = emas[0]["ema"].flatten()
second = emas[1]["ema"].flatten()
bools = np.abs(first[-len(second):] - second)/second < 0.0001
xpoints = np.compress(bools, emas[1])
```

3. Now that we have the crossover points, annotate them with arrows. Make sure that the annotation text is slightly away from the crossover points.

```
for xpoint in xpoints:
    ax.annotate('x', xy=xpoint, textcoords='offset points',
                xytext=(-50, 30),
                arrowprops=dict(arrowstyle="->"))
```

4. Add a legend and let Matplotlib decide where to put it.

```
leg = ax.legend(loc='best', fancybox=True)
```

5. Make the legend transparent by setting the alpha channel value

```
leg.get_frame().set_alpha(0.5)
```

The stock price and moving averages with legend and annotations would appear as follows:

What just happened?

We plotted the close price of a stock and three of its exponential moving averages. We added a legend to the plot. We annotated the crossover points of the first two averages with annotations (see `emalegend.py`):

```
from matplotlib.finance import quotes_historical_yahoo
from matplotlib.dates import DateFormatter
from matplotlib.dates import DayLocator
from matplotlib.dates import MonthLocator
import sys
from datetime import date
import matplotlib.pyplot as plt
import numpy as np

today = date.today()
start = (today.year - 1, today.month, today.day)

symbol = 'DISH'

if len(sys.argv) == 2:
    symbol = sys.argv[1]
```

```
quotes = quotes_historical_yahoo(symbol, start, today)
quotes = np.array(quotes)
dates = quotes.T[0]
close = quotes.T[4]


fig = plt.figure()
ax = fig.add_subplot(111)

emas = []
for i in range(9, 18, 3):
    weights = np.exp(np.linspace(-1., 0., i))
    weights /= weights.sum()

    ema = np.convolve(weights, close)[i-1:-i+1]
    idx = (i - 6)/3
    ax.plot(dates[i-1:], ema, lw=idx, label="EMA(%s)" % (i))
    data = np.column_stack((dates[i-1:], ema))
    emas.append(np.rec.fromrecords(data, names=["dates", "ema"]))

first = emas[0]["ema"].flatten()
second = emas[1]["ema"].flatten()
bools = np.abs(first[-len(second):] - second)/second < 0.0001
xpoints = np.compress(bools, emas[1])

for xpoint in xpoints:
    ax.annotate('x', xy=xpoint, textcoords='offset points',
                xytext=(-50, 30),
                arrowprops=dict(arrowstyle="->"))

leg = ax.legend(loc='best', fancybox=True)
leg.get_frame().set_alpha(0.5)

alldays = DayLocator()
months = MonthLocator()
month_formatter = DateFormatter("%b %Y")
ax.plot(dates, close, lw=1.0, label="Close")
ax.xaxis.set_major_locator(months)
ax.xaxis.set_minor_locator(alldays)
ax.xaxis.set_major_formatter(month_formatter)
ax.grid(True)
fig.autofmt_xdate()
plt.show()
```

Three dimensional plots

Three-dimensional plots are pretty spectacular so we have to cover them here too.
For 3D plots, we need an `Axes3D` object associated with a 3d projection.

Time for action – plotting in three dimensions

We will plot in three dimensions a simple three-dimensional function:

$$z = x^2 + y^2$$

1. We need to use the `3d` keyword to specify a three-dimensional projection for the plot.

   ```
   ax = fig.add_subplot(111, projection='3d')
   ```

2. To create a square two-dimensional grid, we will use the `meshgrid` function. This will be used to initialize the x and y values.

   ```
   u = np.linspace(-1, 1, 100)

   x, y = np.meshgrid(u, u)
   ```

3. We will specify the row strides, column strides, and the color map for the surface plot. The strides determine the size of the "tiles" on the surface. The choice for colormap is a matter of taste.

   ```
   ax.plot_surface(x, y, z,  rstride=4, cstride=4,
   cmap=cm.YlGnBu_r)
   ```

   The result is the following 3D plot:

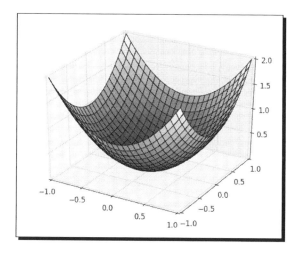

What just happened?

We created a plot of a three dimensional function (see `three_d.py`):

```
from mpl_toolkits.mplot3d import Axes3D
import matplotlib.pyplot as plt
import numpy as np
from matplotlib import cm

fig = plt.figure()
ax = fig.add_subplot(111, projection='3d')

u = np.linspace(-1, 1, 100)

x, y = np.meshgrid(u, u)
z = x ** 2 + y ** 2
ax.plot_surface(x, y, z,  rstride=4, cstride=4, cmap=cm.YlGnBu_r)

plt.show()
```

Contour plots

Matplotlib contour 3D plots come in two flavors—filled and unfilled. We can create normal contour plots with the `contour` function. For the filled contour plots we can use the `contourf` function.

Time for action – drawing a filled contour plot

We will draw a filled contour plot of the three-dimensional mathematical function in the previous Time for Action. The code is also pretty similar. One key difference is that we don't need the 3d projection parameter any more. To draw the filled contour plot we need this line of code:

```
ax.contourf(x, y, z)
```

This gives us the following filled contour plot.

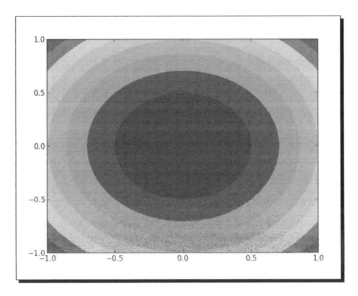

What just happened?

We created a filled contour plot of a three-dimensional mathematical function
(see `contour.py`):

```python
import matplotlib.pyplot as plt
import numpy as np
from matplotlib import cm

fig = plt.figure()
ax = fig.add_subplot(111)

u = np.linspace(-1, 1, 100)

x, y = np.meshgrid(u, u)
z = x ** 2 + y ** 2
ax.contourf(x, y, z)

plt.show()
```

Animation

Matplotlib offers fancy animation capabilities. Matplotlib has a special animation module. We need to define a callback function that is used to regularly update the screen. We also need a function to generate data to be plotted.

Time for action – animating plots

We will plot three random datasets and display them as circles, dots, and triangles. However, we will only update two of those datasets with random values.

1. We will plot 3 random datasets as circles, dots and triangles in different colors.

    ```
    circles, triangles, dots = ax.plot(x, 'ro', y, 'g^', z, 'b.')
    ```

2. This function will get called to update the screen regularly. We will update two of the plots with new y values.

    ```
    def update(data):
        circles.set_ydata(data[0])
        triangles.set_ydata(data[1])
        return circles, triangles
    ```

3. We will generate random data with NumPy.

    ```
    def generate():
        while True: yield np.random.rand(2, N)
    ```

    Here is a snapshot of the animation in action:

What just happened?

We created an animation of random data points (see `animation.py`):

```python
import numpy as np
import matplotlib.pyplot as plt
import matplotlib.animation as animation

fig = plt.figure()
ax = fig.add_subplot(111)
N = 10
x = np.random.rand(N)
y = np.random.rand(N)
z = np.random.rand(N)
circles, triangles, dots = ax.plot(x, 'ro', y, 'g^', z, 'b.')
ax.set_ylim(0, 1)
plt.axis('off')

def update(data):
    circles.set_ydata(data[0])
    triangles.set_ydata(data[1])
    return circles, triangles

def generate():
    while True: yield np.random.rand(2, N)

anim = animation.FuncAnimation(fig, update, generate, interval=150)
plt.show()
```

Summary

This chapter was about Matplotlib—a Python plotting library. We covered simple plots, histograms, plot customization, subplots, 3D plots, contour plots, and logplots. We also saw a few examples of displaying stock charts. Obviously, we only scratched the surface and saw the tip of the iceberg. Matplotlib is very feature rich, so we didn't have space to cover LaTex support, polar coordinates support, and other functionality.

The author of Matplotlib, John Hunter, passed away in August, 2012. One of the technical reviewers of this book suggested mentioning the John Hunter Memorial Fund (http://numfocus.org/johnhunter/). The memorial fund set up by the NumFocus Foundation is an opportunity for us, as fans of John Hunter's work, to "give back" so to say. Again, for more details, check out the previous link to the NumFocus website.

The next chapter is about SciPy—a scientific Python framework that is built on top of NumPy.

10
When NumPy is Not Enough – SciPy and Beyond

SciPy is the world famous Python open-source scientific computing library built on top of NumPy. It adds functionality such as numerical integration, optimization, statistics, and special functions.

In this chapter we will cover the following topics:

- ◆ File I/O
- ◆ Statistics
- ◆ Signal processing
- ◆ Optimization
- ◆ Interpolation
- ◆ Image and audio processing

MATLAB and Octave

MATLAB and its open source alternative Octave are popular mathematical programs. The `scipy.io` package has functions that let you load MATLAB or Octave matrices and arrays of numbers or strings in Python programs and vice versa. The `loadmat` function loads a `.mat` file. The `savemat` function saves a dictionary of names and arrays into a `.mat` file.

Time for action – saving and loading a .mat file

If we start with NumPy arrays and decide to use the said arrays within a MATLAB or Octave environment, the easiest thing to do is create a .mat file. We then can load the file within MATLAB or Octave. Let's go through the necessary steps:

1. Create a NumPy array and call savemat to create a .mat file. This function has two parameters – a filename and a dictionary containing variable names and values.

   ```
   a = np.arange(7)

   io.savemat ("a.mat", {"array": a})
   ```

2. Within a MATLAB or Octave environment, load the .mat file and check the stored array.

   ```
   octave-3.4.0:7> load a.mat
   octave-3.4.0:8> a

   octave-3.4.0:8> array
   array =

      0
      1
      2
      3
      4
      5
      6
   ```

What just happened?

We created a .mat file from NumPy code and loaded it within Octave. We checked the NumPy array that was created (see scipyio.py).

```
import numpy as np
from scipy import io

a = np.arange(7)

io.savemat ("a.mat", {"array": a})
```

Pop quiz – loading .mat files

Q1. Which function loads `.mat` files?

1. `Loadmatlab`
2. `loadmat`
3. `loadoct`
4. `frommat`

Statistics

The SciPy statistics module is called `scipy.stats`. There is one class that implements continuous distributions and one class that implements discrete distributions. Also in this module, functions can be found that can perform a great number of statistical tests.

Time for action – analyzing random values

We will generate random values that mimic a normal distribution and analyze the generated data with statistical functions from the `scipy.stats` package. Perform the following steps to do so:

1. Generate random values from a normal distribution using the `scipy.stats` package.

   ```
   generated = stats.norm.rvs(size=900)
   ```

2. Fit the generated values to a normal distribution. This basically gives us the mean and standard deviation of the data set.

   ```
   print "Mean", "Std", stats.norm.fit(generated)
   ```

   The mean and standard deviation would be shown as follows:

   ```
   Mean Std (0.0071293257063200707, 0.95537708218972528)
   ```

3. Skewness tells us how skewed (asymmetric) a probability distribution is. Perform a skewness test. This test returns two values. The second value is the p-value; the probability that the skewness of the data set corresponds to a normal distribution. The `pvalue` instances range from 0 to 1.

   ```
   print "Skewtest", "pvalue", stats.skewtest(generated)
   ```

   The result of the skewness test would be shown as follows:

   ```
   Skewtest pvalue (-0.62120640688766893, 0.5344638245033837)
   ```

   So there is a 53 percent chance that we are dealing with a normal distribution.

4. Kurtosis tells us how "curved" a probability distribution is. Perform a kurtosis test. This test is set up in a similar way as the skewness test, but of course, applies to kurtosis.

```
print "Kurtosistest", "pvalue",
   stats.kurtosistest(generated)
```

The result of the kurtosis test would be shown as follows:

```
Kurtosistest pvalue (1.3065381019536981, 0.19136963054975586)
```

5. A normality test tells us how likely it is that a data set complies to the normal distribution. Perform a normality test. This test also returns two values, of which the second is the p-value

```
print "Normaltest", "pvalue", stats.normaltest(generated)
```

The result of the normality test would be shown as follows:

```
Normaltest pvalue (2.09293921181506, 0.35117535059841687)
```

6. We can easily find the value at a certain percentile with SciPy.

```
print "95 percentile",
   stats.scoreatpercentile(generated, 95)
```

The value at the 95th percentile would be shown as follows:

```
95 percentile 1.54048860252
```

7. Do the opposite of the previous step to find the percentile at 1.

```
print "Percentile at 1",
   stats.percentileofscore(generated, 1)
```

The percentile at 1 would be shown as follows:

```
Percentile at 1 85.5555555556
```

8. Plot the generated values in a histogram with Matplotlib. More information about Matplotlib can be found in the previous chapter.

```
plt.hist(generated)
plt.show()
```

The following is the histogram of the generated random values:

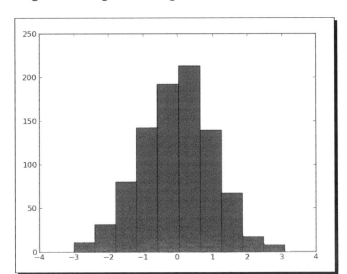

What just happened?

We created a data set from a normal distribution and analyzed it with the `scipy.stats` module (see `statistics.py`).

```
from scipy import stats
import matplotlib.pyplot as plt

generated = stats.norm.rvs(size=900)
print "Mean", "Std", stats.norm.fit(generated)
print "Skewtest", "pvalue", stats.skewtest(generated)
print "Kurtosistest", "pvalue", stats.kurtosistest(generated)
print "Normaltest", "pvalue", stats.normaltest(generated)
print "95 percentile", stats.scoreatpercentile(generated, 95)
print "Percentile at 1", stats.percentileofscore(generated, 1)
plt.hist(generated)
plt.show()
```

Have a go hero – improving the data generation

Judging from the histogram in the *Time for action – analyzing random values* section, there is still room for improvement when it comes to generating the data. Try using NumPy or different parameters of the `scipy.stats.norm.rvs` function.

Samples' comparison and SciKits

Often we will have two data samples, maybe from different experiments, that are somehow related. Statistical tests exist that can compare the samples. Some of these have been implemented in the `scipy.stats` module.

Another statistical test that I like is the Jarque-Bera normality test from `scikits.statsmodels.stattools`. SciKits are small experimental Python software toolkits. They are not part of SciPy. There is also pandas, which is an offshoot of `scikits.statsmodels`. A list of SciKits can be found at `https://scikits.appspot.com/scikits`. You can install `statsmodels` using `setuptools` with the following command:

```
easy_install statsmodels
```

Time for action – comparing stock log returns

We will download the stock quotes for the last year of two trackers using Matplotlib. As mentioned in the previous chapter, we can retrieve quotes from Yahoo! Finance. We will compare the log returns of the close price of DIA and SPY. Also we will perform the Jarque-Bera test on the difference of the log returns. Perform the following steps to do so:

1. Write a function that can return the close price for a specified stock.

```
def get_close(symbol):
    today = date.today()
    start = (today.year - 1, today.month, today.day)

    quotes = quotes_historical_yahoo(symbol, start, today)
    quotes = np.array(quotes)

    return quotes.T[4]
```

2. Calculate the log returns for DIA and SPY. The log returns are calculated by taking the natural logarithm of the close price and then taking the difference of consecutive values.

```
spy = np.diff(np.log(get_close("SPY")))
dia = np.diff(np.log(get_close("DIA")))
```

3. The means comparison test checks whether two different samples could have the same mean value. Two values are returned, of which the second is a p-value from 0 to 1.

```
print "Means comparison", stats.ttest_ind(spy, dia)
```

The result of the means comparison test would be shown as follows:

```
Means comparison (-0.017995865641886155, 0.98564930169871368)
```

So there is about a 98 percent chance that the two samples have the same mean log return.

4. The Kolmogorov-Smirnov two samples test tells us how likely it is that two samples are drawn from the same distribution.

```
print "Kolmogorov smirnov test", stats.ks_2samp(spy, dia)
```

Again, two values are returned of which the second value is the p-value.

```
Kolmogorov smirnov test (0.063492063492063516,
0.67615647616238039)
```

5. Unleash the Jarque-Bera normality test on the difference of the log returns.

```
print "Jarque Bera test",
   jarque_bera(spy - dia)[1]
```

The p-value of the Jarque-Bera normality test would be shown as follows:

```
Jarque Bera test 0.596125711042
```

6. Plot the histograms of the log returns and the difference thereof with Matplotlib.

```
plt.hist(spy, histtype="step", lw=1, label="SPY")
plt.hist(dia, histtype="step", lw=2, label="DIA")
plt.hist(spy - dia, histtype="step", lw=3,
   label="Delta")
plt.legend()
plt.show()
```

The histograms of the log returns and difference are shown in the following screenshot:

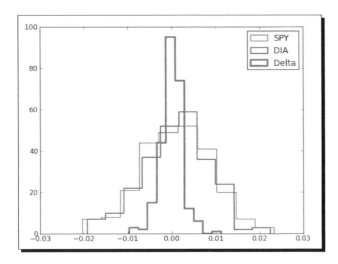

What just happened?

We compared samples of log returns for DIA and SPY. We also performed the Jarque-Bera test on the difference of the log returns (see `pair.py`).

```
from matplotlib.finance import quotes_historical_yahoo
from datetime import date
import numpy as np
from scipy import stats
from statsmodels.stats.stattools import jarque_bera
import matplotlib.pyplot as plt


def get_close(symbol):
    today = date.today()
    start = (today.year - 1, today.month, today.day)

    quotes = quotes_historical_yahoo(symbol, start, today)
    quotes = np.array(quotes)

    return quotes.T[4]

spy =  np.diff(np.log(get_close("SPY")))
dia =  np.diff(np.log(get_close("DIA")))

print "Means comparison", stats.ttest_ind(spy, dia)
print "Kolmogorov smirnov test", stats.ks_2samp(spy, dia)

print "Jarque Bera test", jarque_bera(spy - dia)[1]

plt.hist(spy, histtype="step", lw=1, label="SPY")
plt.hist(dia, histtype="step", lw=2, label="DIA")
plt.hist(spy - dia, histtype="step", lw=3, label="Delta")
plt.legend()
plt.show()
```

Signal processing

The `scipy.signal` module contains filter functions and B-spline interpolation algorithms.

Spline interpolation uses a polynomial called a spline for interpolation. The interpolation then tries to glue splines together to fit the data. B-spline is a type of spline.

A SciPy signal is defined as an array of numbers. An example of a filter is the detrend function. This function takes a signal and does a linear fit on it. This trend is then subtracted from the original input data.

Time for action – detecting a trend in QQQ

Often we are more interested in the trend of a data sample than in detrending it. Still we can get the trend back easily after detrending. Let's do that for 1 year of price data for QQQ:

1. Write code that gets the close price and corresponding dates for QQQ.

```
today = date.today()
start = (today.year - 1, today.month, today.day)

quotes = quotes_historical_yahoo("QQQ", start, today)
quotes = np.array(quotes)

dates = quotes.T[0]
qqq = quotes.T[4]
```

2. Detrend the signal.

```
y = signal.detrend(qqq)
```

3. Create month and day locators for the dates.

```
alldays = DayLocator()
months = MonthLocator ()
```

4. Create a date formatter that creates a string of month name and year.

```
month_formatter = DateFormatter("%b %Y")
```

5. Create a figure and subplot.

```
fig = plt.figure()
ax = fig.add_subplot(111)
```

6. Plot the data and underlying trend by subtracting the detrended signal.

```
plt.plot(dates, qqq, 'o', dates, qqq - y, '-')
```

7. Set the locators and formatter.

```
ax.xaxis.set_minor_locator(alldays)
ax.xaxis.set_major_locator(months)
ax.xaxis.set_major_formatter(month_formatter)
```

8. Format the x-axis labels as dates.

```
fig.autofmt_xdate()
plt.show()
```

The following screenshot shows the QQQ prices with a trend line:

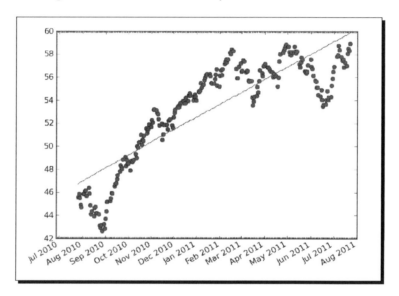

What just happened?

We plotted the closing price for QQQ with a trend line (see `trend.py`).

```
from matplotlib.finance import quotes_historical_yahoo
from datetime import date
import numpy as np
from scipy import signal
import matplotlib.pyplot as plt
from matplotlib.dates import DateFormatter
from matplotlib.dates import DayLocator
from matplotlib.dates import MonthLocator

today = date.today()
start = (today.year - 1, today.month, today.day)
```

```
quotes = quotes_historical_yahoo("QQQ", start, today)
quotes = np.array(quotes)

dates = quotes.T[0]
qqq = quotes.T[4]


y = signal.detrend(qqq)

alldays = DayLocator()
months = MonthLocator()
month_formatter = DateFormatter("%b %Y")

fig = plt.figure()
ax = fig.add_subplot(111)

plt.plot(dates, qqq, 'o', dates, qqq - y, '-')
ax.xaxis.set_minor_locator(alldays)
ax.xaxis.set_major_locator(months)
ax.xaxis.set_major_formatter(month_formatter)
fig.autofmt_xdate()
plt.show()
```

Fourier analysis

Signals in the real world often have a periodic nature. A commonly used tool to deal with these signals is the Fourier transform. The Fourier transform is a transformation from the time domain into the frequency domain, that is, the linear decomposition of a periodic signal into sine and cosine functions with various frequencies.

The functions for Fourier transforms can be found in the `scipy.fftpack` module (NumPy also has its own Fourier package, `numpy.fft`). Included in the package are fast Fourier transforms, differential and pseudo-differential operators, as well as several helper functions. MATLAB users will be pleased to know that a number of functions in the `scipy.fftpack` module have the same names as their MATLAB counterparts and similar functions as their MATLAB equivalents.

Time for action – filtering a detrended signal

We learned in how to detrend a signal in the *Time for action – detecting a trend in QQQ* section. This detrended signal could have a cyclical component. Let's try to visualize this. Some of the steps are a repetition of steps in the previous *Time for action* tutorial, such as downloading the data and setting up Matplotlib objects. These steps are omitted here.

1. Apply Fourier transforms, which will give us the frequency spectrum.

```
amps = np.abs(fftpack.fftshift(fftpack.rfft(y)))
```

2. Filter out the noise. Let's say if the magnitude of a frequency component is below 10 percent of the strongest component, throw it out.

```
amps[amps < 0.1 * amps.max()] = 0
```

3. Transform the filtered signal back to the original domain and plot it together with the detrended signal.

```
plt.plot(dates, y, 'o', label="detrended")
plt.plot(dates,
    -fftpack.irfft(fftpack.ifftshift(amps)),
    label="filtered")
```

4. Format the x-axis labels as dates and add a legend with extra large size.

```
fig.autofmt_xdate()
plt.legend(prop={'size':'x-large'})
```

5. Add a second subplot and plot the frequency spectrum after filtering.

```
ax2 = fig.add_subplot(212)
N = len(qqq)
plt.plot(np.linspace(-N/2, N/2, N), amps,
    label="transformed")
```

6. Display the legend and plot.

```
plt.legend(prop={'size':'x-large'})

plt.show()
```

The following plots are of the signal and frequency spectrum:

What just happened?

We detrended a signal and applied a simple filter on it using the `scipy.fftpack` module (see `frequencies.py`).

```
from matplotlib.finance import quotes_historical_yahoo
from datetime import date
import numpy as np
from scipy import signal
import matplotlib.pyplot as plt
from scipy import fftpack
from matplotlib.dates import DateFormatter
from matplotlib.dates import DayLocator
from matplotlib.dates import MonthLocator


today = date.today()
start = (today.year - 1, today.month, today.day)

quotes = quotes_historical_yahoo("QQQ", start, today)
quotes = np.array(quotes)

dates = quotes.T[0]
qqq = quotes.T[4]
```

```
y = signal.detrend(qqq)

alldays = DayLocator()
months = MonthLocator()
month_formatter = DateFormatter("%b %Y")

fig = plt.figure()
fig.subplots_adjust(hspace=.3)
ax = fig.add_subplot(211)

ax.xaxis.set_minor_locator(alldays)
ax.xaxis.set_major_locator(months)
ax.xaxis.set_major_formatter(month_formatter)

# make font size bigger
ax.tick_params(axis='both', which='major', labelsize='x-large')

amps = np.abs(fftpack.fftshift(fftpack.rfft(y)))
amps[amps < 0.1 * amps.max()] = 0

plt.plot(dates, y, 'o', label="detrended")
plt.plot(dates, -fftpack.irfft(fftpack.ifftshift(amps)),
label="filtered")
fig.autofmt_xdate()
plt.legend(prop={'size':'x-large'})

ax2 = fig.add_subplot(212)
ax2.tick_params(axis='both', which='major', labelsize='x-large')
N = len(qqq)
plt.plot(np.linspace(-N/2, N/2, N), amps, label="transformed")

plt.legend(prop={'size':'x-large'})
plt.show()
```

Mathematical optimization

Optimization algorithms try to find the optimal solution for a problem, for instance finding the maximum or the minimum of a function. The function can be linear or non-linear. The solution could also have special constraints. For example, the solution may not be allowed to have negative values. Several optimization algorithms are provided by the `scipy.optimize` module. One of the algorithms is a least squares fitting function, `leastsq`. When calling this function, we are required to provide a residuals (error terms) function. This function is used to minimize the sum of the squares of the residuals. It corresponds to our mathematical model for the solution. Also, it is necessary to give the algorithm a starting point. This should be a best guess—as close as possible to the real solution. Otherwise, execution will stop after about 800 iterations.

Time for action – fitting to a sine

In the *Time for action – filtering a detrended signal* section we created a simple filter for detrended data. Now let's use a more restrictive filter that will leave us only with the main frequency component. We will fit a sinusoidal pattern to it and plot our results. This model has four parameters—amplitude, frequency, phase, and vertical offset. Perform the following steps to fit to a sine:

1. Define a `residuals` function based on a sine wave model.

    ```
    def residuals(p, y, x):
        A,k,theta,b = p
        err = y-A * np.sin(2* np.pi* k * x + theta) + b

        return err
    ```

2. Transform the filtered signal back to the original domain.

    ```
    filtered = -fftpack.irfft(fftpack.ifftshift(amps))
    ```

3. Guess the values of the parameters for which we are trying to estimate a transformation from the time domain into the frequency domain.

    ```
    N = len(qqq)
    f = np.linspace(-N/2, N/2, N)
    p0 = [filtered.max(), f[amps.argmax()]/(2*N), 0, 0]
    print "P0", p0
    ```

    The initial values would be shown as follows:

    ```
    P0 [2.6679532410065212, 0.00099598469163686377, 0, 0]
    ```

4. Call the `leastsq` function.

    ```
    plsq = optimize.leastsq(residuals, p0, args=(filtered,
      dates))
    p = plsq[0]
    print "P", p
    ```

    The following are the final parameter values:

    ```
    P [  2.67678014e+00   2.73033206e-03  -8.00007036e+03
    -5.01260321e-03]
    ```

5. Finish the first subplot with detrended data, filtered data, and fit of the filtered data. Use a date format for the horizontal axis and add a legend.

```
plt.plot(dates, y, 'o', label="detrended")
plt.plot(dates, filtered, label="filtered")
plt.plot(dates, p[0] * np.sin(2 * np.pi *
    dates * p[1] + p[2]) + p[3], '^', label="fit")
fig.autofmt_xdate()
plt.legend(prop={'size':'x-large'})
```

6. Add a second subplot with a legend of the main component of the frequency spectrum.

```
ax2 = fig.add_subplot(212)
plt.plot(f, amps, label="transformed")
```

The following shows the resulting charts:

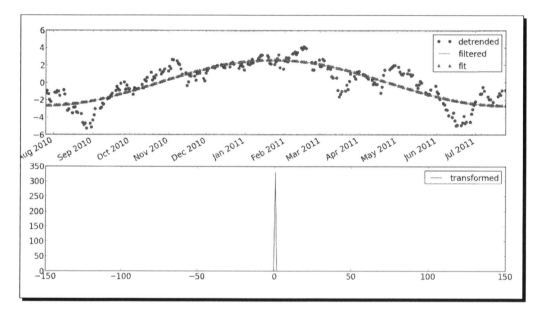

What just happened?

We detrended 1 year of price data for QQQ. This signal was then filtered until only the main component of the frequency spectrum was left over. We fitted a sine to the filtered signal using the scipy.optimize module (see optfit.py).

```
from matplotlib.finance import quotes_historical_yahoo
import numpy as np
import matplotlib.pyplot as plt
```

```
from scipy import fftpack
from scipy import signal
from matplotlib.dates import DateFormatter
from matplotlib.dates import DayLocator
from matplotlib.dates import MonthLocator
from scipy import optimize

start = (2010, 7, 25)
end = (2011, 7, 25)

quotes = quotes_historical_yahoo("QQQ", start, end)
quotes = np.array(quotes)

dates = quotes.T[0]
qqq = quotes.T[4]

y = signal.detrend(qqq)


alldays = DayLocator()
months = MonthLocator()
month_formatter = DateFormatter("%b %Y")

fig = plt.figure()
fig.subplots_adjust(hspace=.3)
ax = fig.add_subplot(211)

ax.xaxis.set_minor_locator(alldays)
ax.xaxis.set_major_locator(months)
ax.xaxis.set_major_formatter(month_formatter)
ax.tick_params(axis='both', which='major', labelsize='x-large')

amps = np.abs(fftpack.fftshift(fftpack.rfft(y)))
amps[amps < amps.max()] = 0

def residuals(p, y, x):
    A,k,theta,b = p
    err = y-A * np.sin(2* np.pi* k * x + theta) + b

    return err

filtered = -fftpack.irfft(fftpack.ifftshift(amps))
N = len(qqq)
f = np.linspace(-N/2, N/2, N)
```

```
p0 = [filtered.max(), f[amps.argmax()]/(2*N), 0, 0]
print "P0", p0

plsq = optimize.leastsq(residuals, p0, args=(filtered, dates))
p = plsq[0]
print "P", p
plt.plot(dates, y, 'o', label="detrended")
plt.plot(dates, filtered, label="filtered")
plt.plot(dates, p[0] * np.sin(2 * np.pi * dates * p[1] + p[2]) + p[3],
'^', label="fit")
fig.autofmt_xdate()
plt.legend(prop={'size':'x-large'})

ax2 = fig.add_subplot(212)
ax2.tick_params(axis='both', which='major', labelsize='x-large')
plt.plot(f, amps, label="transformed")

plt.legend(prop={'size':'x-large'})
plt.show()
```

Numerical integration

SciPy has a numerical integration package, `scipy.integrate`, which has no equivalent in NumPy. The `quad` function can integrate a one-variable function between two points. These points can be at infinity. The function uses the simplest numerical integration method, the trapezoid rule.

Time for action – calculating the Gaussian integral

The Gaussian integral is related to the `error` function (also known as erf in mathematics), but has no finite limits. It evaluates to the square root of pi. Let's calculate the integral with the `quad` function.

Calculate the Gaussian integral with the `quad` function.

```
print "Gaussian integral", np.sqrt(np.pi),
integrate.quad(lambda x: np.exp(-x**2),
-np.inf, np.inf)
```

The return value is the outcome and its error would be shown as follows:

Gaussian integral 1.77245385091 (1.7724538509055159, 1.4202636780944923e-08)

What just happened?

We calculated the Gaussian integral with the `quad` function.

Interpolation

Interpolation "fills in the blanks" between known data points in a data set. The `scipy.interpolate` function interpolates a function based on experimental data. The `interp1d` class can create a linear or cubic interpolation function. By default a linear interpolation function is constructed, but if the `kind` parameter is set, a cubic interpolation function is created instead. The `interp2d` class works the same way, but in 2D.

Time for action – interpolating in one dimension

We will create data points using a `sinc` function and add some random noise to them. After that, we will do a linear and cubic interpolation, and plot the results. Perform the following steps to do so:

1. Create the data points and add noise to them.

```
x = np.linspace(-18, 18, 36)
noise = 0.1 * np.random.random(len(x))
signal = np.sinc(x) + noise
```

2. Create a linear interpolation function and apply it to an input array with five times as many data points.

```
interpreted = interpolate.interp1d(x, signal)
x2 = np.linspace(-18, 18, 180)
y = interpreted(x2)
```

3. Do the same as in the previous step, but with cubic interpolation.

```
cubic = interpolate.interp1d(x, signal, kind="cubic")
y2 = cubic(x2)
```

4. Plot the results with Matplotlib.

```
plt.plot(x, signal, 'o', label="data")
plt.plot(x2, y, '-', label="linear")
plt.plot(x2, y2, '-', lw=2, label="cubic")

plt.legend()
plt.show()
```

The following screenshot is a plot of the data, linear, and cubic interpolation:

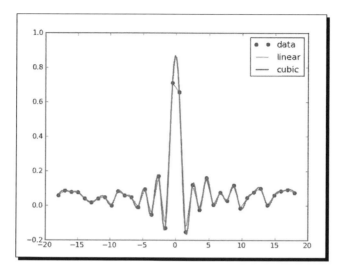

What just happened?

We created a data set from the `sinc` function and added noise to it. We then did linear and cubic interpolation using the `interp1d` class of the `scipy.interpolate` module (see `sincinterp.py`).

```
import numpy as np
from scipy import interpolate
import matplotlib.pyplot as plt

x = np.linspace(-18, 18, 36)
noise = 0.1 * np.random.random(len(x))
signal = np.sinc(x) + noise

interpreted = interpolate.interp1d(x, signal)
x2 = np.linspace(-18, 18, 180)
y = interpreted(x2)

cubic = interpolate.interp1d(x, signal, kind="cubic")
y2 = cubic(x2)

plt.plot(x, signal, 'o', label="data")
plt.plot(x2, y, '-', label="linear")
plt.plot(x2, y2, '-', lw=2, label="cubic")

plt.legend()
plt.show()
```

Image processing

With SciPy, we can do image processing using the `scipy.ndimage` package. The module contains various image filters and utilities.

Time for action – manipulating Lena

In the `scipy.misc` module, there is a utility that loads the image of "Lena". This is the image of Lena Soderberg traditionally used for image processing examples. We will apply some filters on this image and rotate it. Perform the following steps to do so:

1. Load the "Lena" image and display it in a subplot with grayscale colormap.

```
image = misc.lena().astype(np.float32)

plt.subplot(221)
plt.title("Original Image")
img = plt.imshow(image, cmap=plt.cm.gray)
```

Note that we are dealing with a `float32` array.

2. The median filter scans the signal and replaces each item by the median of neighboring data points. Apply a median filter to the image and display it in a second subplot.

```
plt.subplot(222)
plt.title("Median Filter")
filtered = ndimage.median_filter(image, size=(42,42))
plt.imshow(filtered, cmap=plt.cm.gray)
```

3. Rotate the image and display it in the third subplot.

```
plt.subplot(223)
plt.title("Rotated")
rotated = ndimage.rotate(image, 90)
plt.imshow(rotated, cmap=plt.cm.gray)
```

4. The Prewitt filter is based on computing the gradient of image intensity. Apply a Prewitt filter to the image and display it in the fourth subplot.

```
plt.subplot(224)
plt.title("Prewitt Filter")
filtered = ndimage.prewitt(image)
plt.imshow(filtered, cmap=plt.cm.gray)
plt.show()
```

The following are the resulting images:

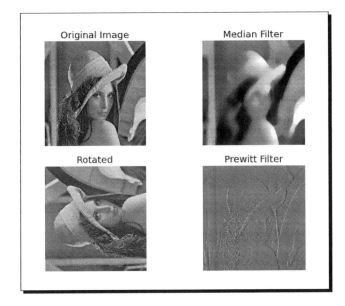

What just happened?

We manipulated the image of "Lena" in several ways using the `scipy.ndimage` module (see `images.py`).

```
from scipy import misc
import numpy as np
import matplotlib.pyplot as plt
from scipy import ndimage


image = misc.lena().astype(np.float32)

plt.subplot(221)
plt.title("Original Image")
img = plt.imshow(image, cmap=plt.cm.gray)
plt.axis("off")

plt.subplot(222)
plt.title("Median Filter")
filtered = ndimage.median_filter(image, size=(42,42))
plt.imshow(filtered, cmap=plt.cm.gray)
plt.axis("off")
```

```
plt.subplot(223)
plt.title("Rotated")
rotated = ndimage.rotate(image, 90)
plt.imshow(rotated, cmap=plt.cm.gray)
plt.axis("off")

plt.subplot(224)
plt.title("Prewitt Filter")
filtered = ndimage.prewitt(image)
plt.imshow(filtered, cmap=plt.cm.gray)
plt.axis("off")
plt.show()
```

Audio processing

Now that we have done some image processing, you will probably be not surprised that we can do exciting things with WAV files too. Let's download a WAV file and replay it a couple of times. We will skip the explanation of the download part, which is just regular Python.

Time for action – replaying audio clips

We will download a WAV file of Austin Powers exclaiming "Smashing, baby!". This file can be converted to a NumPy array with the read function from the scipy.io.wavfile module. The write function from the same package will be used to create a new WAV file at the end of this tutorial. We will further use the tile function to replay the audio clip several times. Perform the following steps to do so:

1. Read the file with the read function.

    ```
    sample_rate, data = wavfile.read(WAV_FILE)
    ```

    This gives us two items – sample rate and audio data. For this tutorial we are only interested in the audio data.

2. Apply the tile function.

    ```
    repeated = np.tile(data, int(sys.argv[1]))
    ```

3. Write a new file with the write function.

    ```
    wavfile.write("repeated_yababy.wav",
        sample_rate, repeated)
    ```

The original audio data and the audio clip repeated four times are shown in the following plot:

What just happened?

We read an audio clip, repeated it four times and then created a new WAV file with the new array (see `repeat_audio.py`).

```
from scipy.io import wavfile
import matplotlib.pyplot as plt
import urllib2
import numpy as np
import sys


response = urllib2.urlopen('http://www.thesoundarchive.com/
austinpowers/smashingbaby.wav')
print response.info()
WAV_FILE = 'smashingbaby.wav'
filehandle = open(WAV_FILE, 'w')
filehandle.write(response.read())
filehandle.close()
sample_rate, data = wavfile.read(WAV_FILE)
print "Data type", data.dtype, "Shape", data.shape

plt.subplot(2, 1, 1)
plt.title("Original")
```

```
plt.plot(data)

plt.subplot(2, 1, 2)

# Repeat the audio fragment
repeated = np.tile(data, int(sys.argv[1]))

# Plot the audio data
plt.title("Repeated")
plt.plot(repeated)
wavfile.write("repeated_yababy.wav",
    sample_rate, repeated)

plt.show ()
```

Summary

In this chapter we only scratched the surface of what is possible with SciPy and SciKits. Still, we learned a bit about file I/O, statistics, signal processing, optimization, interpolation, and audio and image processing.

In the next chapter we will create some simple, yet fun, games with Pygame – the open-source Python game library. During this process we will learn about NumPy integration with Pygame, a machine learning Scikits module and more.

11

Playing with Pygame

This chapter is for developers who want to create games with NumPy and Pygame quickly and easily. Basic game development experience would help but isn't necessary.

In this chapter we will cover the following topics:

- Pygame basics
- Matplotlib integration
- Surface pixel arrays
- Artificial intelligence
- Animation
- OpenGL

Pygame

Pygame is a Python framework originally written by Pete Shinners, which, as its name suggests, can be used to create video games. Pygame is free, open source since 2004 and licensed under the General Public License, which means that you are allowed to basically make any type of game. Pygame is built on top of the **Simple DirectMedia Layer (SDL)**. SDL is a C framework that gives access to graphics, sound, keyboard, and other input devices on various operating systems including Linux, Mac OS X, and Windows.

Time for action – installing Pygame

We will install Pygame in this tutorial. Pygame should be compatible with all Python versions. At the time of writing there were some incompatibility issues with Python 3, but in all probability, these will be fixed soon. Perform the following steps to install Pygame:

1. Depending on the operating system, you have the following options with which you install Pygame:

    - **Debian and Ubuntu**: Pygame can be found in the Debian archives at `http://packages.qa.debian.org/p/pygame.html`.

    - **Windows**: From the Pygame website (`http://www.pygame.org/download.shtml`) we can download the appropriate binary installer for the Python version we are using.

    - **Mac**: Binary Pygame packages for Mac OS X 10.3 and up can be found at `http://www.pygame.org/download.shtml`.

2. Pygame uses the `distutils` system for compiling and installing. To start installing Pygame with the default options, simply run the following command:

    `python setup.py`

    If you need more information about the available options, type:

    `python setup.py help`

3. In order to compile the code, you need to have a compiler for your operating system. Setting this up is beyond the scope of this book. More information about compiling Pygame on Windows can be found at `http://pygame.org/wiki/CompileWindows`. More information about compiling Pygame on Mac OS X can be found at `http://pygame.org/wiki/MacCompile`.

Hello World

We will create a simple game that we will further improve later in this chapter. As is traditional in books about programming, we will start with a "Hello World" example.

Time for action – creating a simple game

It's important to notice the so-called main game loop where all the action happens and the usage of the `Font` module to render text. In this program we will manipulate a Pygame `Surface` object that is used for drawing, and we will handle a quit event. Perform the following steps to create a simple game:

1. First import the required Pygame modules. If Pygame is installed properly, we should get no errors, otherwise please return to the installation recipe.

```
import pygame, sys
from pygame.locals import *
```

2. We will initialize Pygame, create a display of 400 x 300 pixels, and set the window title to **Hello World!**.

```
pygame.init()
screen = pygame.display.set_mode((400, 300))

pygame.display.set_caption('Hello World!')
```

3. Games usually have a game loop, which runs forever until for instance a quit event occurs. In this example we will only set a label with the text **Hello World** at coordinates `(100, 100)`. **The text has font size of** `19` **and a red color.**

```
while True:
    sysFont = pygame.font.SysFont("None", 19)
    rendered = sysFont.render
    ('Hello World', 0, (255, 100, 100))
    screen.blit(rendered, (100, 100))

    for event in pygame.event.get():
      if event.type == QUIT:
        pygame.quit()
        sys.exit()

    pygame.display.update()
```

We get the following screenshot as an end result:

The following is the complete code for the "Hello World" example:

```
import pygame, sys
from pygame.locals import *

pygame.init()
screen = pygame.display.set_mode((400, 300))

pygame.display.set_caption('Hello World!')

while True:
    sysFont = pygame.font.SysFont("None", 19)
    rendered = sysFont.render
    ('Hello World', 0, (255, 100, 100))
    screen.blit(rendered, (100, 100))

    for event in pygame.event.get():
      if event.type == QUIT:
        pygame.quit()
        sys.exit()

    pygame.display.update()
```

What just happened?

It might not seem like much, but we learned a lot in this tutorial. The functions that passed the review are summarized in the following table:

Function	Description
`pygame.init()`	This function does initialization and needs to be called before other Pygame functions are called.
`pygame.display.set_mode((400, 300))`	This creates a so-called `Surface` object to draw on. We give this function a tuple representing the dimensions of the surface.
`pygame.display.set_caption('Hello World!')`	This sets the window title to a specified string value.
`pygame.font.SysFont("None", 19)`	This creates a system font from a comma-separated list of fonts (in this case. none) and a font size parameter.
`sysFont.render('Hello World', 0, (255, 100, 100))`	This draws text on a `Surface` object. The last parameter is a tuple representing the RGB values of a color.

Function	Description
`screen.blit(rendered, (100, 100))`	This draws on a `Surface` object.
`pygame.event.get()`	This gets a list of `Event` objects. The `Event` objects represent some special occurrence in the system, such as a user quitting the game.
`pygame.quit()`	This cleans up resources used by Pygame. Call this function before exiting the game.
`pygame.display.update()`	This refreshes the surface.

Animation

Most games, even the most static ones, have some level of animation. From a programmer's standpoint, animation is nothing more than displaying an object at a different place at a different time, thus simulating movement.

Pygame offers a `Clock` object, which manages how many frames are drawn per second. This ensures that animation is independent of how fast the user's CPU is.

Time for action – animating objects with NumPy and Pygame

We will load an image and use NumPy again to define a clockwise path around the screen. Perform the following steps to do so:

1. We can create a Pygame clock, as follows:

```
clock = pygame.time.Clock()
```

2. As part of the source code accompanying this book, there should be a picture of a head. We will load this image and move it around on the screen.

```
img = pygame.image.load('head.jpg')
```

3. We will define some arrays to hold the coordinates of the positions where we would like to put the image during the animation. Since the object will be moved, there are four logical sections of the path – right, down, left, and up. Each of these sections will have 40 equidistant steps. We will initialize all the values in these sections to 0.

```
steps = np.linspace(20, 360, 40).astype(int)
right = np.zeros((2, len(steps)))
down = np.zeros((2, len(steps)))
left = np.zeros((2, len(steps)))
up = np.zeros((2, len(steps)))
```

4. It's trivial to set the coordinates of the positions of the image. However, there is one tricky bit to be aware of – the `[::-1]` notation leads to reversing the order of the array elements.

```
right[0] = steps
right[1] = 20

down[0] = 360
down[1] = steps

left[0] = steps[::-1]
left[1] = 360

up[0] = 20
up[1] = steps[::-1]
```

5. The path sections can be joined, but before we can do this, the arrays have to be transposed with the `T` operator, because they are not aligned properly for concatenation.

```
pos = np.concatenate((right.T, down.T, left.T, up.T))
```

6. In the main event loop we will set the clock tick at a rate of 30 frames per second:

```
clock.tick(30)
```

The following is a screenshot of the moving head:

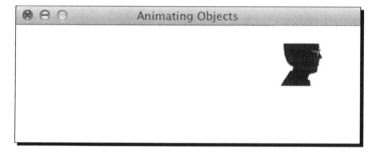

You should be able to watch a movie of this animation at https://www.youtube.com/watch?v=m2TagGiq1fs.

The code of this example uses almost everything we learned so far, but should still be simple enough to understand:

```
import pygame, sys
from pygame.locals import *
import numpy as np
```

```
pygame.init()
clock = pygame.time.Clock()
screen = pygame.display.set_mode((400, 400))

pygame.display.set_caption('Animating Objects')
img = pygame.image.load('head.jpg')

steps = np.linspace(20, 360, 40).astype(int)
right = np.zeros((2, len(steps)))
down = np.zeros((2, len(steps)))
left = np.zeros((2, len(steps)))
up = np.zeros((2, len(steps)))

right[0] = steps
right[1] = 20

down[0] = 360
down[1] = steps

left[0] = steps[::-1]
left[1] = 360

up[0] = 20
up[1] = steps[::-1]

pos = np.concatenate((right.T, down.T, left.T, up.T))
i = 0

while True:
    # Erase screen
    screen.fill((255, 255, 255))

    if i >= len(pos):
      i = 0

    screen.blit(img, pos[i])
    i += 1

    for event in pygame.event.get():
      if event.type == QUIT:
        pygame.quit()
        sys.exit()

    pygame.display.update()
    clock.tick(30)
```

What just happened?

We learned a bit about animation in this tutorial. The most important concept we learned about, is about the clock. The new functions that we used are described in the following table:

Function	Description
`pygame.time.Clock()`	This creates a game clock.
`clock.tick(30)`	This executes a "tick" of the game clock. Here `30` is the number of frames per second.

Matplotlib

Matplotlib is an open-source library for easy plotting that we learned about in *Chapter 9, Plotting with Matplotlib*. We can integrate Matplotlib into a Pygame game and create various plots.

Time for action – using Matplotlib in Pygame

In this recipe we will take the position coordinates of the previous tutorial and make a graph from them. Perform the following steps to do so:

1. Using a noninteractive backend: In order to integrate Matplotlib with Pygame we need to use a noninteractive backend, otherwise Matplotlib will present us with a GUI window by default. We will import the main Matplotlib module and call the use function. This function has to be called immediately after importing the main Matplotlib module and before other Matplotlib modules are imported.

```
import matplotlib as mpl

mpl.use("Agg")
```

2. Noninteractive plots can be drawn on a Matplotlib canvas. Creating this canvas requires imports, creating a figure and a subplot. We will specify the figure to be 3 x 3 inches large. More details can be found at the end of this section.

```
import matplotlib.pyplot as plt
import matplotlib.backends.backend_agg as agg

fig = plt.figure(figsize=[3, 3])
ax = fig.add_subplot(111)
canvas = agg.FigureCanvasAgg(fig)
```

3. In noninteractive mode, plotting data is a bit more complicated than in the default mode. Since we need to plot repeatedly, it makes sense to organize the plotting code in a function. The plot is eventually drawn on the canvas. The canvas adds a bit of complexity to our setup. At the end of this example you can find a more detailed explanation of the functions.

```
def plot(data):
    ax.plot(data)
    canvas.draw()
    renderer = canvas.get_renderer()

    raw_data = renderer.tostring_rgb()
    size = canvas.get_width_height()

    return pygame.image.fromstring(raw_data, size, "RGB")
```

The following screenshot shows the animation in action. You can also view a screencast on YouTube at `https://www.youtube.com/watch?v=t6qTeXxtnl4.`

4. We get the following code after the changes:

```
import pygame, sys
from pygame.locals import *
import numpy as np
import matplotlib as mpl

mpl.use("Agg")
```

```
import matplotlib.pyplot as plt
import matplotlib.backends.backend_agg as agg

fig = plt.figure(figsize=[3, 3])
ax = fig.add_subplot(111)
canvas = agg.FigureCanvasAgg(fig)

def plot(data):
    ax.plot(data)
    canvas.draw()
    renderer = canvas.get_renderer()

    raw_data = renderer.tostring_rgb()
    size = canvas.get_width_height()

    return pygame.image.fromstring(raw_data, size, "RGB")

pygame.init()
clock = pygame.time.Clock()
screen = pygame.display.set_mode((400, 400))

pygame.display.set_caption('Animating Objects')
img = pygame.image.load('head.jpg')

steps = np.linspace(20, 360, 40).astype(int)
right = np.zeros((2, len(steps)))
down = np.zeros((2, len(steps)))
left = np.zeros((2, len(steps)))
up = np.zeros((2, len(steps)))

right[0] = steps
right[1] = 20

down[0] = 360
down[1] = steps

left[0] = steps[::-1]
left[1] = 360

up[0] = 20
up[1] = steps[::-1]

pos = np.concatenate((right.T, down.T, left.T, up.T))
```

```
i = 0
history = np.array([])
surf = plot(history)

while True:
    # Erase screen
    screen.fill((255, 255, 255))

    if i >= len(pos):
        i = 0
        surf = plot(history)

    screen.blit(img, pos[i])
    history = np.append(history, pos[i])
    screen.blit(surf, (100, 100))

    i += 1

    for event in pygame.event.get():
        if event.type == QUIT:
            pygame.quit()
            sys.exit()

    pygame.display.update()
    clock.tick(30)
```

What just happened?

The plotting-related functions are explained in the following table:

Function	Description
`mpl.use("Agg")`	This specifies the use of the noninteractive backend.
`plt.figure(figsize=[3, 3])`	This creates a figure of 3 x 3 inches.
`agg.FigureCanvasAgg(fig)`	This creates a canvas in noninteractive mode.
`canvas.draw()`	This draws on the canvas.
`canvas.get_renderer()`	This gets a renderer for the canvas.

Surface pixels

The Pygame `surfarray` module handles the conversion between Pygame `Surface` objects and NumPy arrays. As you may recall, NumPy can manipulate big arrays in a fast and efficient manner.

Time for action – accessing surface pixel data with NumPy

In this tutorial we will tile a small image to fill the game screen. Perform the following steps to do so:

1. The `array2d` function copies pixels into a two-dimensional array. There is a similar function for three-dimensional arrays. We will copy the pixels from the avatar image into an array:

```
pixels = pygame.surfarray.array2d(img)
```

2. Let's create the game screen from the shape of the `pixels` array using the `shape` attribute of the array. The screen will be seven times larger in both directions.

```
X = pixels.shape[0] * 7
Y = pixels.shape[1] * 7
screen = pygame.display.set_mode((X, Y))
```

3. Tiling the image is easy with the NumPy `tile` function. The data needs to be converted to integer values, since colors are defined as integers.

```
new_pixels = np.tile(pixels, (7, 7)).astype(int)
```

4. The `surfarray` module has a special function (`blit_array`) to display the array on the screen.

```
pygame.surfarray.blit_array(screen, new_pixels)
```

This produces the following screenshot:

The following code does the tiling of the image:

```
import pygame, sys
from pygame.locals import *
import numpy as np

pygame.init()
img = pygame.image.load('head.jpg')
pixels = pygame.surfarray.array2d(img)
X = pixels.shape[0] * 7
Y = pixels.shape[1] * 7
screen = pygame.display.set_mode((X, Y))
pygame.display.set_caption('Surfarray Demo')
new_pixels = np.tile(pixels, (7, 7)).astype(int)

while True:
    screen.fill((255, 255, 255))
    pygame.surfarray.blit_array(screen, new_pixels)

    for event in pygame.event.get():
      if event.type == QUIT:
          pygame.quit()
          sys.exit()

    pygame.display.update()
```

What just happened?

The following is a brief description of the new functions and attributes we used:

Function	Description
pygame.surfarray.array2d(img)	This copies pixel data into a 2D array.
pygame.surfarray.blit_array(screen, new_pixels)	This displays array values on the screen.

Artificial intelligence

Often we need to mimic intelligent behavior within a game. The scikit-learn project aims to provide an API for machine learning. What I like the most about it is the amazing documentation. We can install scikit-learn with the package manager of our operating system. This option may or may not be available depending on the operating system, but should be the most convenient route. Windows users can just download an installer from the project website.

On Debian and Ubuntu the project is called `python-sklearn`. On MacPorts the ports are called `py26-scikits-learn` and `py27-scikits-learn`. We can also install from source or using `easy_install`. There are third-party distributions from Python(x, y) – Enthought and NetBSD.

We can install `scikit-learn` by typing in the following command at the command line:

```
pip install -U scikit-learn
```

Or you can also do it with the following command:

```
easy_install -U scikit-learn
```

This might not work because of permissions, so you may need to put `sudo` in front of the commands or log in as an admin.

Time for action – clustering points

We will generate some random points and cluster them, which means that points that are close to each other are put in the same cluster. This is only one of the many techniques that you can apply with `scikit-learn`. Clustering is a type of machine learning algorithm, which aims to group items based on similarities. Second, we will calculate a square affinity matrix. An affinity matrix is a matrix containing affinity values; for instance, distances between points. Finally, we will cluster the points with the `AffinityPropagation` class from `scikit-learn`. Perform the following steps to cluster points:

1. We will generate 30 random point positions within a square of 400 x 400 pixels:

    ```
    positions = np.random.randint(0, 400, size=(30, 2))
    ```

2. We will use the Euclidean distance to the origin as affinity matrix.

    ```
    positions_norms = np.sum(positions ** 2, axis=1)
    S = - positions_norms[:, np.newaxis] - positions_norms[np.newaxis,
    :] + 2 * np.dot(positions, positions.T)
    ```

3. Give the `AffinityPropagation` class the result from the previous step. This class labels the points with the appropriate cluster number.

    ```
    aff_pro = sklearn.cluster.AffinityPropagation().fit(S)
    labels = aff_pro.labels_
    ```

4. We will draw polygons for each cluster. The function involved requires a list of points, a color (let's paint it red), and a surface.

    ```
    pygame.draw.polygon(screen, (255, 0, 0), polygon_points[i])
    ```

The result is a bunch of polygons for each cluster, as shown in the following screenshot:

The clustering example code is as follows:

```
import numpy as np
import sklearn.cluster
import pygame, sys
from pygame.locals import *

positions = np.random.randint(0, 400, size=(30, 2))

positions_norms = np.sum(positions ** 2, axis=1)
S = - positions_norms[:, np.newaxis] - positions_norms[np.newaxis,
:] + 2 * np.dot(positions, positions.T)

aff_pro = sklearn.cluster.AffinityPropagation().fit(S)
labels = aff_pro.labels_

polygon_points = []

for i in xrange(max(labels) + 1):
    polygon_points.append([])

# Sorting points by cluster
for i in xrange(len(labels)):
    polygon_points[labels[i]].append(positions[i])
```

```
pygame.init()
screen = pygame.display.set_mode((400, 400))

while True:
    for i in xrange(len(polygon_points)):
        pygame.draw.polygon(screen, (255, 0, 0), polygon_points[i])

    for event in pygame.event.get():
        if event.type == QUIT:
            pygame.quit()
            sys.exit()

    pygame.display.update()
```

What just happened?

The most important lines in the artificial intelligence example are described in more detail in the following table:

Function	Description
`sklearn.cluster.AffinityPropagation().fit(S)`	This creates an `AffinityPropagation` object and performs a fit using an affinity matrix.
`pygame.draw.polygon(screen, (255, 0, 0), polygon_points[i])`	This draws a polygon given a surface, a color (red in this case), and a list of points.

OpenGL and Pygame

OpenGL specifies an API for 2D and 3D computer graphics. The API consists of functions and constants. We will be concentrating on the Python implementation called PyOpenGL. Install PyOpenGL with the following command:

pip install PyOpenGL PyOpenGL_accelerate

You might need to have root access to execute this command. The following is the corresponding `easy_install` command:

easy_install PyOpenGL PyOpenGL_accelerate

Time for action – drawing the Sierpinski gasket

For the purpose of demonstration we will draw a Sierpinski gasket, also known as Sierpinski triangle or Sierpinski Sieve with OpenGL. This is a fractal pattern in the shape of a triangle created by the mathematician Waclaw Sierpinski. The triangle is obtained via a recursive and, in principle, infinite procedure. Perform the following steps to draw the Sierpinski gasket:

1. First, we will start out by initializing some of the OpenGL-related primitives. This includes setting the display mode and background color. A line-by-line explanation is given at the end of this section.

```
def display_openGL(w, h):
    pygame.display.set_mode((w,h),
    pygame.OPENGL|pygame.DOUBLEBUF)

    glClearColor(0.0, 0.0, 0.0, 1.0)
    glClear(GL_COLOR_BUFFER_BIT|GL_DEPTH_BUFFER_BIT)

    gluOrtho2D(0, w, 0, h)
```

2. The algorithm requires us to display points, the more the better. First, we set the drawing color to red. Second, we define the vertices (I call them points myself) of a triangle. Then we define random indices, which are to be used to choose one of the three triangle vertices. We pick a random point somewhere in the middle – it doesn't really matter where. After that we draw points halfway between the previous point and one of the vertices picked at random. Finally, we "flush" the result.

```
glColor3f(1.0, 0, 0)
vertices = np.array([[0, 0], [DIM/2, DIM], [DIM, 0]])
NPOINTS = 9000
indices = np.random.random_integers(0, 2, NPOINTS)
point = [175.0, 150.0]

for i in xrange(NPOINTS):
    glBegin(GL_POINTS)
    point = (point + vertices
    [indices[i]])/2.0
    glVertex2fv(point)
    glEnd()

glFlush()
```

The Sierpinski triangle looks like the following screenshot:

The following is the full Sierpinski gasket demo code with all the imports:

```python
import pygame
from pygame.locals import *
import numpy as np

from OpenGL.GL import *
from OpenGL.GLU import *

def display_openGL(w, h):
    pygame.display.set_mode((w,h), pygame.OPENGL|pygame.DOUBLEBUF)

    glClearColor(0.0, 0.0, 0.0, 1.0)
    glClear(GL_COLOR_BUFFER_BIT|GL_DEPTH_BUFFER_BIT)


    gluOrtho2D(0, w, 0, h)

def main():
    pygame.init()
    pygame.display.set_caption('OpenGL Demo')
    DIM = 400
    display_openGL(DIM, DIM)
    glColor3f(1.0, 0, 0)
    vertices = np.array([[0, 0], [DIM/2, DIM], [DIM, 0]])
    NPOINTS = 9000
    indices = np.random.random_integers(0, 2, NPOINTS)
    point = [175.0, 150.0]

    for i in xrange(NPOINTS):
```

```
            glBegin(GL_POINTS)
            point = (point + vertices[indices[i]])/2.0
            glVertex2fv(point)
            glEnd()

        glFlush()
        pygame.display.flip()

        while True:
            for event in pygame.event.get():
                if event.type == QUIT:
                    return

    if __name__ == '__main__':
        main()
```

What just happened?

As promised, the following is a line-by-line explanation of the most important parts of the example:

Function	Description
`pygame.display.set_mode((w,h), pygame.OPENGL|pygame.DOUBLEBUF)`	This sets the display mode to the required width, height, and OpenGL display.
`glClear(GL_COLOR_BUFFER_BIT|GL_DEPTH_BUFFER_BIT)`	This clears the buffers using a mask. Here we clear the color buffer and depth buffer bits.
`gluOrtho2D(0, w, 0, h)`	This defines a 2D orthographic projection matrix with the coordinates of the left, right, top, and bottom clipping planes.
`glColor3f(1.0, 0, 0)`	This defines the current drawing color using three float values for RGB. In this case we will be painting in red.
`glBegin(GL_POINTS)`	This delimits the vertices of primitives or a group of primitives. Here the primitives are points.
`glVertex2fv(point)`	This renders a point given a vertex.
`glEnd()`	This closes a section of code started with `glBegin`.
`glFlush()`	This forces execution of GL commands.

Simulation game with PyGame

As a last example, we will simulate life with Conway's Game of Life. The original game of life is based on a few basic rules. We start out with a random configuration on a two-dimensional square grid. Each cell in the grid can be either dead or alive. This state depends on the eight neighbors of the cell. Convolution can be used to evaluate the basic rules of the game. We will need the SciPy package for the convolution process.

Time for action – simulating life

The following code is an implementation of Game of Life with some modifications, as follows:

- ◆ Clicking once with the mouse draws a cross until we click again
- ◆ Pressing the *r* key resets the grid to a random state
- ◆ Pressing *b* creates blocks based on the mouse position
- ◆ Pressing *g* creates gliders

The most important data structure in the code is a two-dimensional array holding the color values of the pixels on the game screen. This array is initialized with random values and then recalculated for each iteration of the game loop. More information about the involved functions can be found in the next section.

1. To evaluate the rules, we will use convolution, as follows.

```
def get_pixar(arr, weights):
    states = ndimage.convolve(arr, weights, mode='wrap')

    bools = (states == 13) | (states == 12 ) | (states == 3)

    return bools.astype(int)
```

2. We can draw a cross using basic indexing tricks that we learned in *Chapter 2, Beginning with NumPy Fundamentals*.

```
def draw_cross(pixar):
    (posx, posy) = pygame.mouse.get_pos()
    pixar[posx, :] = 1
    pixar[:, posy] = 1
```

3. Initialize the grid with random values:

```
def random_init(n):
    return np.random.random_integers(0, 1, (n, n))
```

The following is the code in its entirety:

```
import os, pygame
from pygame.locals import *
import numpy as np
from scipy import ndimage

def get_pixar(arr, weights):
  states = ndimage.convolve(arr, weights, mode='wrap')

  bools = (states == 13) | (states == 12 ) | (states == 3)

  return bools.astype(int)

def draw_cross(pixar):
    (posx, posy) = pygame.mouse.get_pos()
    pixar[posx, :] = 1
    pixar[:, posy] = 1

def random_init(n):
    return np.random.random_integers(0, 1, (n, n))

def draw_pattern(pixar, pattern):
     print pattern

    if pattern == 'glider':
      coords = [(0,1), (1,2), (2,0), (2,1), (2,2)]
    elif pattern == 'block':
      coords = [(3,3), (3,2), (2,3), (2,2)]
    elif pattern == 'exploder':
      coords = [(0,1), (1,2), (2,0), (2,1), (2,2), (3,3)]
    elif pattern == 'fpentomino':
      coords = [(2,3),(3,2),(4,2),(3,3),(3,4)]

    pos = pygame.mouse.get_pos()

    xs = np.arange(0, pos[0], 10)
    ys = np.arange(0, pos[1], 10)

    for x in xs:
        for y in ys:
            for i, j in coords:
                pixar[x + i, y + j] = 1
```

```
def main():
    pygame.init ()
    N = 400
    pygame.display.set_mode((N, N))
    pygame.display.set_caption("Life Demo")

    screen = pygame.display.get_surface()

    pixar = random_init(N)
    weights = np.array([[1,1,1], [1,10,1], [1,1,1]])

    cross_on = False

    while True:
        pixar = get_pixar(pixar, weights)

        if cross_on:
            draw_cross(pixar)

        pygame.surfarray.blit_array(screen, pixar * 255 ** 3)
        pygame.display.flip()

        for event in pygame.event.get():
            if event.type == QUIT:
                return
            if event.type == MOUSEBUTTONDOWN:
                cross_on = not cross_on
            if event.type == KEYDOWN:
                if event.key == ord('r'):
                    pixar = random_init(N)
                    print "Random init"
                if event.key == ord('g'):
                    draw_pattern(pixar, 'glider')
                if event.key == ord('b'):
                    draw_pattern(pixar, 'block')
                if event.key == ord('e'):
                    draw_pattern(pixar, 'exploder')
                if event.key == ord('f'):
                    draw_pattern(pixar, 'fpentomino')

if __name__ == '__main__':
    main()
```

You should able to view a screencast on YouTube at `https://www.youtube.com/watch?v=NNsU-yWTkXM`. The following is a screenshot of the game in action:

What just happened?

We used some NumPy and SciPy functions that need an explanation, as follows:

Function	Description
`ndimage.convolve(arr, weights, mode='wrap')`	This applies the `convolve` operation on the given array, using weights in wrap mode. The mode has to do it with the array borders.
`bools.astype(int)`	This converts the array of Booleans to integers.
`np.arange(0, pos[0], 10)`	This creates an array from 0 to `pos[0]` in steps of 10. So if `pos[0]` is equal to 1000, we will get 0, 10, 20, ..., 990.

Summary

You might have found the mention of Pygame in this book a bit odd. After reading this chapter I hope you realized that NumPy and Pygame go well together. Games, after all, involve lots of computation for which NumPy and SciPy are ideal choices. They also require artificial intelligence capabilities as found in `scikit-learn`. Anyway, making games is fun and we hope this last chapter was the equivalent of a nice dessert or coffee after a ten-course meal. If you are still hungry for more, please check out *NumPy Cookbook, Ivan Idris, Packt Publishing*; it builds further on this book with minimum overlap.

Pop Quiz Answers

Chapter 1, NumPy Quick Start

What does `arrange(5)` do?	It creates a NumPy array with values 0 to 4.
	The created NumPy array has values 0, 1, 2, 3, 4.

Chapter 2, Beginning with NumPy Fundamentals

How is the shape of an `ndarray` stored?	It is stored in a tuple.

Chapter 3, Get into Terms with Commonly Used Functions

Which function returns the weighted average of an array?	`average`

Chapter 4, Convenience functions for your convenience

Which function returns the covariance of two arrays?	`cov`

Chapter 5, Working with Matrices and ufuncs

What is the row delimiter in a string accepted by the `mat` and `bmat` functions?	Semicolon

Chapter 6, Move further with NumPy modules

Which function can create matrices?	`mat`

Chapter 7, Peeking into special routines

Which NumPy module deals with random numbers?	`random`

Chapter 8, Assure Quality with Testing

Which parameter of the `assert_almost_equal` function specifies the decimal precision?	`decimal`

Chapter 9, Plotting with Matplotlib

What does the `plot` function do?	It does neither 1, 2, or 3.

Chapter 10, When NumPy is not enough Scipy and beyond

Which function loads `.mat` files?	`loadmat`

Index

Thank you for buying
Numpy Beginner's Guide

About Packt Publishing

Packt, pronounced 'packed', published its first book "*Mastering phpMyAdmin for Effective MySQL Management*" in April 2004 and subsequently continued to specialize in publishing highly focused books on specific technologies and solutions.

Our books and publications share the experiences of your fellow IT professionals in adapting and customizing today's systems, applications, and frameworks. Our solution based books give you the knowledge and power to customize the software and technologies you're using to get the job done. Packt books are more specific and less general than the IT books you have seen in the past. Our unique business model allows us to bring you more focused information, giving you more of what you need to know, and less of what you don't.

Packt is a modern, yet unique publishing company, which focuses on producing quality, cutting-edge books for communities of developers, administrators, and newbies alike. For more information, please visit our website: www.packtpub.com.

About Packt Open Source

In 2010, Packt launched two new brands, Packt Open Source and Packt Enterprise, in order to continue its focus on specialization. This book is part of the Packt Open Source brand, home to books published on software built around Open Source licences, and offering information to anybody from advanced developers to budding web designers. The Open Source brand also runs Packt's Open Source Royalty Scheme, by which Packt gives a royalty to each Open Source project about whose software a book is sold.

Writing for Packt

We welcome all inquiries from people who are interested in authoring. Book proposals should be sent to author@packtpub.com. If your book idea is still at an early stage and you would like to discuss it first before writing a formal book proposal, contact us; one of our commissioning editors will get in touch with you.

We're not just looking for published authors; if you have strong technical skills but no writing experience, our experienced editors can help you develop a writing career, or simply get some additional reward for your expertise.

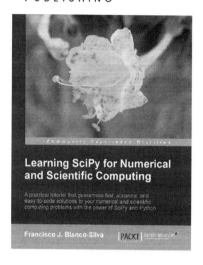

Learning SciPy for Numerical and Scientific Computing

ISBN: 978-1-78216-162-2   Paperback: 150 pages

A practical tutorial that guarantees fast, accurate, and easy-to-code solutions to your numerical and scientific computing problems with the power of SciPy and Python

1. Perform complex operations with large matrices, including eigenvalue problems, matrix decompositions, or solution to large systems of equations

2. Step-by-step examples to easily implement statistical analysis and data mining that rivals in performance any of the costly specialized software suites

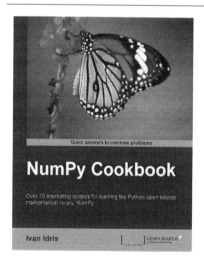

NumPy Cookbook

ISBN: 978-1-84951-892-5   Paperback: 226 pages

Over 70 interesting recipes for learning the Python open source mathematical library, NumPy

1. Do high performance calculations with clean and efficient NumPy code

2. Analyze large sets of data with statistical functions

3. Execute complex linear algebra and mathematical computations

Please check **www.PacktPub.com** for information on our titles

open source
community experience distilled

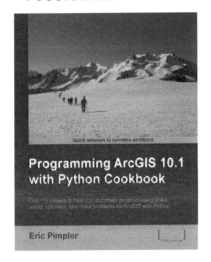

Programming ArcGIS 10.1 with Python Cookbook

ISBN: 978-1-84969-444-5   Paperback: 304 pages

Over 75 recipes to help you automate geoprocessing tasks, create solutions, and solve problems for ArcGIS with Python

1. Learn how to create geoprocessing scripts with ArcPy

2. Customize and modify ArcGIS with Python

3. Create time-saving tools and scripts for ArcGIS

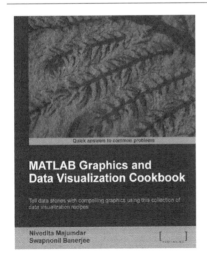

MATLAB Graphics and Data Visualization Cookbook

ISBN: 978-1-84969-316-5   Paperback: 284 pages

Tell data stories with compelling graphics using this collection of data visualization recipes

1. Collection of data visualization recipes with functionalized versions of common tasks for easy integration into your data analysis workflow

2. Recipes cross-referenced with MATLAB product pages and MATLAB Central File Exchange resources for improved coverage

3. Includes hand created indices to find exactly what you need; such as application driven, or functionality driven solutions

Please check **www.PacktPub.com** for information on our titles

30234369R00175

Made in the USA
Lexington, KY
24 February 2014